The Stories Behind

Old-Time BASEBALL TRIVIA

KERRY BANKS

GREY*S*TONE BOOKS

DOUGLAS & McINTYRE
VANCOUVER/TORONTO/NEW YORK

For my father, Edward, who took me to my first ballgame.

Copyright © 1999 by Kerry Banks

99 00 01 02 03   5 4 3 2 1

All rights reserved. No part of this book may be reproduced, stored in a retrieval system or transmitted in any form or by any means, without the prior permission of the publisher or, in the case of photocopying or other reprographic copying, a licence from CANCOPY (Canadian Reprography Collective), Toronto, Ontario.

Greystone Books
A division of Douglas & McIntyre Ltd.
2323 Quebec Street, Suite 201
Vancouver, British Columbia V5T 4S7

Canadian Cataloguing in Publication Data

Banks, Kerry, 1952–
   The stormy years 1969–89

   ISBN 1-55054-673-2

   1. Baseball—History—Miscellanea. I. Title
GV867.3.B36 1999   796.357′09   C99-910018-1

Editing by John Eerkes
Cover and text design by Peter Cocking
Front cover photograph by Malcolm Emmons/*The Sporting News*
Back cover photograph courtesy National Baseball Hall of Fame Library, Cooperstown, N.Y.
Printed and bound in Canada by Transcontinental Printing and Graphics, Inc.

Every reasonable effort has been taken to trace the ownership of copyrighted visual material. Information that will enable the publisher to rectify any reference or credit is welcome.

The publisher gratefully acknowledges the support of the Canada Council for the Arts and of the British Columbia Ministry of Tourism, Small Business and Culture. The publisher also acknowledges the financial support of the Government of Canada through the Book Publishing Industry Development Program for its publishing activities.

Contents

PREFACE

The era began in 1969, with the underdog New York Mets' miraculous march to glory. It ended with another supernatural occurrence—an earthquake that caused a ten-day halt in the 1989 World Series between the Oakland Athletics and the San Francisco Giants. Yet even before those tremors struck, baseball's foundations had already been shaken by the events of this stormy era.

The first salvo was fired in 1970, when Curt Flood challenged baseball's reserve clause. Although Flood lost his case in the courts, the battle did not end there. In 1976, players won the right to become free agents, and by the end of the decade seven-figure contracts were common. As players' salaries increased, so did attendance. The event many cited as most responsible for rekindling the public's imagination was the thrilling 1975 World Series between the Cincinnati Reds and the Boston Red Sox, which drew 70 million TV viewers. But that epic clash was only one of the era's highlights. Fans would also witness several historic milestones, including Hank Aaron breaking Babe Ruth's all-time home-run record, Frank Robinson becoming the majors' first black manager, Pete Rose eclipsing Ty Cobb's career hit mark and Nolan Ryan deposing Walter Johnson as the game's strikeout king.

Change was the period's only constant. Some of the innovations were benign: designated hitters, artificial turf, expansion into Canada, league-championship playoffs and World Series broadcasts in prime time. But the era also had a darker legacy: two players' strikes, two umpires' strikes, contract collusion by baseball's owners, a trial at which a parade of players confessed to illegal drug use and the lifetime suspension of Pete Rose for gambling.

There was never a time like it before. It is unlikely there will be another like it again.

KERRY BANKS
January 1999

1

Rickey
Henderson:
He never met a
base that he
couldn't steal.

Chapter One

LEADING OFF

The best leadoff hitter in baseball history was born on Christmas Day in Chicago in 1957. His name is Rickey Henderson. No other player has ever combined speed, power, aggression, base-stealing skills and the ability to get on base in such a dynamic package. An offensive catalyst for every team on which he has played, Henderson has paced his league in thefts a record 12 times and has scored 100 runs 13 times. He has more walks than anyone not named Babe Ruth or Ted Williams, and his lifetime average of .80 runs per game is the highest since Joe DiMaggio. The dust still hasn't settled on Henderson's career, but when it does there will be a plaque waiting for him in Cooperstown.

In this first chapter we lead off with a potpourri of questions about the era from 1969 to 1989. *(Answers are on page 8)*

1.1 Which Hall of Famer hit the most career homers?
A. Mike Schmidt
B. Frank Robinson
C. Reggie Jackson
D. Harmon Killebrew

1.2 **Who was the first Yankee manager to be fired by George Steinbrenner?**
A. Ralph Houk
B. Bill Virdon
C. Clyde King
D. Billy Martin

1.3 **Pete Rose scored the winning run at the 1970 All-Star Game in dramatic style, by slamming into which catcher in a violent collision at home plate?**
A. Carlton Fisk of the Red Sox
B. Ray Fosse of the Indians
C. Bill Freehan of the Tigers
D. Thurman Munson of the Yankees

1.4 **Who did President Richard Nixon describe in 1972 as "the most underpaid player in baseball"?**
A. Vida Blue
B. Brooks Robinson
C. Steve Carlton
D. Johnny Bench

1.5 **Which team was broadcaster Harry Caray working for when he began serenading fans with his rendition of "Take Me Out to the Ballgame"?**
A. The Chicago Cubs
B. The St. Louis Cardinals
C. The Chicago White Sox
D. The Baltimore Orioles

1.6 **Nolan Ryan never topped his league in which pitching category?**
A. ERA
B. Wins
C. Losses
D. Complete games

1.7   **What did Reggie Jackson do in a game on April 15, 1972, that had not been done in the majors since 1914?**
A. He hit two inside-the-park homers
B. He wore a uniform without a number
C. He took the field wearing a mustache
D. He made an unassisted double play in the outfield

1.8   **Minnie Minoso is the oldest player to get a base hit in a major-league game. How old was Minoso when he got his last hit?**
A. 44
B. 47
C. 50
D. 53

1.9   **Who was baseball's first free agent?**
A. Don Gullett
B. Reggie Jackson
C. Catfish Hunter
D. Andy Messersmith

1.10   **What was manager Sparky Anderson's nickname?**
A. "Captain Quip"
B. "Captain Crunch"
C. "Captain Hook"
D. "Captain Midnight"

1.11   **Which pitcher registered the most 20-win seasons?**
A. Tom Seaver
B. Steve Carlton
C. Jim Palmer
D. Ferguson Jenkins

1.12   **Who stole 689 bases in his career without ever leading his league in thefts?**
A. Joe Morgan
B. Cesar Cedeno
C. Davey Lopes
D. Willie Wilson

1.13 In 1976, commissioner Bowie Kuhn refused to allow Oakland Athletics owner Charlie Finley to sell which two players to the Boston Red Sox?

A. Vida Blue and Reggie Jackson

B. Joe Rudi and Rollie Fingers

C. Mike Torrez and Ken Holtzman

D. Sal Bando and Bert Campenaris

1.14 During the 1970s, shortstop Mario Mendoza became associated with what baseball statistic?

A. A high error total

B. A high strikeout total

C. A low batting average

D. A low RBI rate

1.15 Who holds the record for most combined homers and steals in a season, with a minimum of 20 homers?

A. Joe Morgan

B. Eric Davis

C. Bobby Bonds

D. Rickey Henderson

1.16 The AL adopted the designated hitter in 1973. In what year did a DH first appear in a World Series game?

A. 1973

B. 1976

C. 1979

D. 1982

1.17 Who is the oldest player to collect five hits in a game?

A. Pete Rose

B. Lou Brock

C. Carl Yastrzemski

D. Roberto Clemente

1.18 Which NL manager twice removed his starting pitchers from games in which they had no-hitters after eight innings?
A. Danny Ozark
B. Chuck Tanner
C. Preston Gomez
D. Dick Williams

1.19 Who was the first pitcher to win 100 games without ever logging enough innings in a season to qualify for an ERA title?
A. Hoyt Wilhelm
B. Sparky Lyle
C. Mike Marshall
D. Rollie Fingers

1.20 Which team had four of its players sent to jail in 1983 for possessing and selling cocaine?
A. The Kansas City Royals
B. The Cleveland Indians
C. The Pittsburgh Pirates
D. The Philadelphia Phillies

1.21 The Dowd Report was an investigation of what?
A. Salary collusion among baseball's owners
B. Pete Rose's gambling habits
C. George Steinbrenner's relationship with a blackmailer
D. The legality of baseball's reserve clause

Answers

LEADING OFF

1.1   B. Frank Robinson
Although only three players—Hank Aaron, Babe Ruth and Willie Mays—have hit more home runs than Robinson, he is not commonly perceived as one of the long-ball greats. This may be because he led his league in homers only once: in 1966, when he clouted 49 for the Baltimore Orioles, which was also the only season in which he topped the 40-homer plateau. Yet, the perception is clearly not supported by reality—Robinson went deep 586 times.

1.2   B. Bill Virdon
Shipping magnate George Steinbrenner promised "absentee ownership" when he bought the New York Yankees in 1973, saying he would not meddle in the day-to-day affairs of the club, but rather "stick to building ships." It was an empty promise. In his first 20 years as owner, Steinbrenner changed managers 18 times. The first to leave was Ralph Houk, but Houk was not fired—he resigned after the 1973 season. Virdon was the first to get the ax, when he was replaced by Billy Martin on August 1, 1975.

1.3   B. Ray Fosse of the Indians
The 1970 All-Star Game was deadlocked 4–4 in the bottom of the 12th when Jim Hickman singled to center, sending Pete Rose, who had been on second, tearing toward home. As Ray Fosse came out to receive the throw from outfielder Amos Otis, Rose lowered his shoulder and barreled into the catcher like a runaway freight train. While Fosse lay dazed in the dirt, Rose rolled over and touched the plate. His run won the contest for the National League, and the

8

play became symbolic of Rose's gung-ho approach to the game. Fosse suffered an injured shoulder in the collision and was never the same again. Although criticized in some quarters for being overly aggressive in what was essentially an exhibition game, Rose was unrepentant. As he said later, "I could never have looked my father in the eye if I hadn't hit Fosse that day."

1.4 A. Vida Blue

Richard Nixon's observation that Blue was underpaid was right on the money. In 1971, the A's sensational southpaw not only won the AL Cy Young Award, he was also the league's biggest gate attraction. Yet Blue earned only $14,750 that year. After the 1971 season Blue got himself an agent, who asked A's owner Charlie Finley for $95,000. When Finley rejected that demand, offering only $40,000, Blue became an official holdout. The standoff lasted until May 1, 1972, when Blue capitulated, signing for close to Finley's original figure. When he did return, the young hurler bitterly claimed that "Charlie Finley has soured my stomach for baseball." Out of shape and distracted, Blue had a nightmarish year, posting only six wins and becoming a target of the boo birds.

1.5 C. The Chicago White Sox

Although most closely identified with the Chicago Cubs, Harry Caray broadcast games for several other teams, starting with the Cardinals in the 1940s. It was in 1975, while working for the Chicago White Sox, that Caray began crooning his famous off-key rendition of "Take Me Out to the Ballgame" during the seventh-inning stretch. The idea for the stunt came from White Sox owner Bill Veeck. Caray took his act to the Cubs in 1982.

1.6 B. Wins

Despite compiling 319 career wins, Nolan Ryan never led his league in victories. His best year was with the California Angels in 1974, when he won 22 games, but he actually came closest to topping the league in 1977, when he notched 19 victories, one behind Jim Palmer, Dennis Leonard and Dave Goltz. Ryan won ERA titles in 1981 and 1987, led the league in losses with 18 in 1976 and led in complete games with 22 in 1977.

1.7   **C. He took the field wearing a mustache**

When Reggie Jackson reported to spring training in 1972, he was sporting a beard and a mustache. Jackson figured he would encounter resistance to his unshaven look, but Oakland A's owner Charlie Finley sensed a promotional opportunity. Finley surprised Jackson and his teammates by offering everyone $300 if they would grow mustaches. The players eagerly complied and Oakland's distinctive hirsute look was born. When Jackson took the field on Opening Day, it marked the first time since catcher Wally Schang in 1914 that a major leaguer had worn facial hair.

1.8   **D. 53**

On September 11, 1976, Minnie Minoso, who last played in the majors in 1964, suited up as the designated hitter for the Chicago White Sox versus the California Angels. The 53-year-old went hitless in three at-bats. Back in the lineup as DH the next day, Minoso singled off Sid Monge to become the oldest player to hit safely in the majors. In 1980, at age 57, the Cuban returned to make two pinch-hit appearances for the Pale Hose. Although he failed to get a hit, Minoso joined Nick Altrock as the only two players with careers that spanned five decades.

1.9   **C. Catfish Hunter**

When Charlie Finley reneged on Hunter's 1974 contract by failing to pay a $50,000 life-insurance fund annuity, the Players Association filed a grievance on Hunter's behalf, insisting that because of the violation he should be released from his contract. Arbitrator Peter Seitz agreed, and on December 13, 1974, Hunter became baseball's first free agent. After a furious bidding war, he signed a five-year, $3.75 million contract with the Yankees. That was three times the salary of any other major leaguer, and it ushered in an era of skyrocketing salaries.

1.10   **C. "Captain Hook"**

Sparky Anderson was called "Captain Hook" because of his propensity for removing his starting pitchers from games at the first hint of trouble. Four times during the 1970s, his staff in Cincinnati posted the fewest complete games in the NL. However, it's also true

Jim Palmer: He won three Cy Young Awards in a four-year span.

that Anderson's Cincinnati teams did not possess the strongest crop of starters. After he moved to the AL to manage Detroit in 1979, Anderson allowed more of his starters to go the distance, although when the Tigers took the pennant in 1984 his staff racked up only 19 complete games, a paltry sum for a team that won 104 games.

1.11   C. Jim Palmer
The tall right-hander with the loose-jointed windup and fluid delivery was the stud of the Baltimore Orioles staff for more than a decade. Palmer won more games (186) and notched more shutouts (54) than any pitcher during the 1970s. He also posted eight 20-win seasons, tops among modern-day hurlers, and tied with Lefty Grove for the second-most in AL history, behind Walter Johnson.

1.12   **A. Joe Morgan**
No player has stolen as many bases as Morgan without leading his
league in thefts at least once. However, this was due more to the
intense level of competition in the NL than to any fault of Morgan's.
He was the runner-up in stolen bases in seven seasons, five times to
Lou Brock and twice to Davey Lopes.

1.13   **B. Joe Rudi and Rollie Fingers**
Charlie Finley and baseball commissioner Bowie Kuhn were often
at loggerheads during the 1970s. One notable run-in occurred in
1976, when, faced with the prospect of losing some of his star players to free agency, Finley sold Joe Rudi and Rollie Fingers to the
Red Sox for $1 million apiece and Vida Blue to the Yankees for $1.5
million. A few days later Kuhn negated the sales, claiming they
were "not in the best interests of baseball." Finley angrily dubbed
Kuhn "the village idiot." The A's owner later apologized to the village idiots of America, saying that Kuhn was "the nation's idiot."

1.14   **C. A low batting average**
The "Mendoza Line" is an imaginary boundary in batting averages
used to denote poor hitters. It was named for shortstop Mario
Mendoza, who batted below .200 in five of his nine seasons from
1974 to 1982. Coining of the term is credited to George Brett, who
once said, "The first thing I look for in the Sunday papers is to
see who is below the Mendoza line." When Mendoza was in the
majors, the line was simply whatever his batting average happened
to be at the time; nowadays the term usually refers to the .200
mark. Strangely, after his retirement, Mendoza was hired as a
minor-league hitting instructor by the California Angels.

1.15   **D. Rickey Henderson**
Henderson added another element to his already impressive offensive arsenal after being traded to the New York Yankees in 1985:
home-run power. In 1985 and 1986, he stroked 24 and 28 dingers,
while retaining his famous jump on the basepaths. His combined
total of 115 homers and stolen bases in 1986 is the best ever by a
player with 20 homers or more. In fact, Henderson owns three of
the top four totals in the category.

COMBINED HOMERS AND STOLEN BASES (MINIMUM 20 HR)*

Player	Year	Team	HR	SB	Total
Rickey Henderson	1986	Yankees	28	87	115
Eric Davis	1986	Reds	27	80	107
Rickey Henderson	1985	Yankees	24	80	104
Rickey Henderson	1990	Athletics	28	65	93
Joe Morgan	1973	Reds	26	67	93
Alex Rodriguez	1998	Mariners	42	46	88
Eric Davis	1987	Reds	37	50	87
Joe Morgan	1976	Reds	27	60	87

*CURRENT TO 1998

1.16 B. 1976

Although the AL introduced the designated hitter in 1973, it was not until 1976 that teams were allowed to use a DH in the World Series, and then only in even years. Cincinnati's Dan Driessen became the first National Leaguer to take a turn as DH, when he flied out against Yankees pitcher Doyle Alexander in the second inning of game one of the 1976 Series.

1.17 A. Pete Rose

On August 11, 1986, playing against the San Francisco Giants, 45-year-old Pete Rose put a punctuation mark on his star-studded career by cranking out five hits for the tenth time, breaking the NL record he had shared with Max Carey. Rose's last plate appearance came a week later on August 17. The Reds legend left the game with an all-time record 4,256 career hits.

1.18 C. Preston Gomez

Gomez had no special affinity for pitchers. On July 21, 1970, he pulled San Diego Padres starter Clay Kirby for a pinch-hitter in the bottom of the eighth inning with his team trailing 1–0, even though Kirby was working on a no-hitter. The Padres failed to score, and the Mets added two more runs in the ninth for a 3–0 win. On September 4, 1974, while managing the Houston Astros, Gomez

13

removed pitcher Don Wilson for a pinch-hitter in the top of the ninth inning of a scoreless tie with the Reds, even though Wilson had not allowed a hit. The strategy failed to produce a run, but the Reds broke up the no-hitter against Houston's relief staff. Gomez's hard-nosed approach would have made more sense if either of his teams were involved in a pennant race, but both were also-rans.

1.19 D. Rollie Fingers

A distinctive black handlebar mustache lent Fingers the look of an old-west gunfighter and he had the mentality to match. Excelling in pressure-laden, one-on-one showdowns, he posted a record six saves in World Series play. Fingers was the first pitcher to notch 300 career saves, and as of 1998, he is still the only moundsman to earn 100 wins without working enough innings to qualify for an ERA title. His 114–118 career won–lost record is noteworthy for another reason: aside from Satchel Paige, Fingers is the only pitcher to make the Hall of Fame with a sub-.500 winning percentage.

1.20 A. The Kansas City Royals

The Royals were not the only team with a drug problem during the 1980s, but they were the only one to have four players arrested for selling and using cocaine. Willie Wilson, Vida Blue, Willie Aikens and Jerry Martin all served three-month jail terms in 1983 after a plea-bargaining deal reduced their charges from felonies to misdemeanors. Baseball commissioner Bowie Kuhn tried to suspend the four players for a year, but an arbitration panel upheld the penalty only against Blue, who was named as the source of the drugs. In 1984, Wilson was back with the Royals, Aikens joined the Blue Jays and Martin suited up for the Mets.

1.21 B. Pete Rose's gambling habits

The 225-page report, prepared by investigator John Dowd at the behest of baseball commissioner Bart Giamatti, stated that Rose had bet on baseball and football games, horse races and boxing matches, losing as much as $500,000 in a year. Rose allegedly bet on his own team, the Cincinnati Reds, 52 times in 1987 alone, wagering a minimum of $10,000 a day. On August 24, 1989, after weighing the evidence, Giamatti banished Rose from baseball for life.

BASEBALL TITLES

The association between ballplayers and sportwriters is often an uneasy one. Sportswriter Jimmy Cannon called it "a cop-and-crook relationship." Eventually, though, there comes a time when a player needs a writer to help him tell his story. Match the player with the title of his autobiography.   *(Answers are on page 139)*

1.	Nolan Ryan	A. *If at First*
2.	Hank Aaron	B. *The Wrong Stuff*
3.	Bob Gibson	C. *Between the Lines*
4.	Orel Hershiser	D. *Catcher in the Wry*
5.	Tug McGraw	E. *Stranger to the Game*
6.	Bill Lee	F. *Screwball*
7.	Steve Howe	G. *I Had a Hammer*
8.	Ron LeFlore	H. *Throwing Heat*
9.	Bob Uecker	I. *Out of the Blue*
10.	Keith Hernandez	J. *Breakout*
11.	Denny McLain	K. *Say Hey*
12.	Willie Mays	L. *Nobody's Perfect*

Hank Aaron: Just running out all his homers would cover 52 miles.

Chapter Two

KINGS OF SWING

Early in 1965, the Los Angeles Dodgers pitching staff was discussing strategies for handling the heavy hitters they would face in the coming year: Willie Mays, Frank Robinson, Willie McCovey, Dick Allen. When they reached Hank Aaron's name, the room went silent. "Make sure," someone finally said, "there's no one on when he hits it out." Pitchers never did discover how to shut down the shy Alabaman with the rattlesnake-quick wrists. In a 20-year span from 1955 to 1974, Aaron *averaged* 36 homers per season. It was Aaron's amazing longevity and sustained excellence that enabled him to hit more homers than anyone in history. Other players have had more spectacular seasons, but no one else has been able to hit the ball so hard for so long. *(Answers are on page 21)*

2.1 **On April 8, 1974, Hank Aaron blasted his 715th homer to break Babe Ruth's record. Who caught the record-breaking ball?**

A. A fan

B. A hot dog vendor

C. A baseball player

D. A member of the grounds crew

2.2 At what age did Hank Aaron have his best home-run hitting season?
A. 28
B. 31
C. 34
D. 37

2.3 Who retired with 16 games left to play in the 1974 season, yet still won the AL home-run title?
A. Dick Allen of the White Sox
B. Boog Powell of the Orioles
C. George Scott of the Brewers
D. Harmon Killebrew of the Twins

2.4 Who compiled the most career homers in major-league history without ever hitting 30 round-trippers in a season?
A. Al Kaline
B. Steve Garvey
C. Graig Nettles
D. Brooks Robinson

2.5 In 1980, George Brett hit .390, the highest average since Ted Williams batted .406 in 1941. Which statement about Brett's stellar season is false?
A. He had more homers than strikeouts
B. He ranked among the AL's top ten in hits
C. He led the AL in slugging average
D. He was batting above .400 in September

2.6 Which player hit a mammoth home run at the 1971 All-Star Game that struck a light tower on the roof of Tiger Stadium?
A. Reggie Jackson
B. Frank Howard
C. Johnny Bench
D. Willie McCovey

2.7 **Who set one record and tied another by belting five home runs and knocking in 13 runs in a 1972 doubleheader?**
A. Tony Perez of the Reds
B. Nate Colbert of the Padres
C. Bobby Murcer of the Yankees
D. John Mayberry of the Royals

2.8 **Which team connected for a single-game record of ten homers?**
A. The 1975 Cincinnati Reds
B. The 1978 Los Angeles Dodgers
C. The 1982 Milwaukee Brewers
D. The 1987 Toronto Blue Jays

2.9 **Who is the only player to hit 35 homers or more and collect 200 hits in three straight seasons?**
A. Jim Rice
B. Dave Parker
C. Dale Murphy
D. Andre Dawson

2.10 **In 1982, the Mets' Dave Kingman set a record for the lowest batting average by a league home-run champ. What did Kingman hit?**
A. .204
B. .224
C. .244
D. .264

2.11 **Who was the first player to rack up 40-homer seasons in both leagues?**
A. Dave Kingman
B. Frank Robinson
C. Darrell Evans
D. Dave Winfield

2.12 **Which slugger belted four homers in four consecutive at-bats in a single game in 1976?**
A. Jim Rice
B. Bobby Bonds
C. Mike Schmidt
D. Richie Zisk

2.13 **Who hit the first grand-slam homer at an All-Star Game?**
A. Fred Lynn
B. Eddie Murray
C. Gary Carter
D. Pedro Guerrero

2.14 **Who clubbed 40 homers in 1973 to establish a record for the most four-baggers by a player with less than 400 at-bats?**
A. Hank Aaron
B. Johnny Bench
C. Reggie Jackson
D. Willie Stargell

2.15 **Who holds the record for most homers and RBI by a player in his final season?**
A. Rico Carty
B. Bob Horner
C. Dave Kingman
D. Roberto Clemente

2.16 **The two leagues produced 42 home-run champions in the 21 years between 1969 and 1989. How many of these 42 home-run titles were won by players who hit less than 40 homers?**
A. Five
B. Ten
C. 15
D. 20

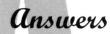

KINGS OF SWING

2.1 **C. A baseball player**

The Atlanta Braves were offering a $25,000 reward to the lucky spectator who caught Aaron's 715th homer. But instead of landing in the hands of a fan, the historic ball cleared the left-field fence at Fulton County Stadium and went into the bullpen, where it was caught on the fly by Atlanta relief pitcher Tom House. As Aaron circled the bases, House sprinted in to deliver the ball to his teammate. When he got there, Aaron was surrounded by a mob of well-wishers near home plate. House shouted, "Hammer, here it is," and put the ball in Aaron's hand. "Thanks kid," replied Aaron and affectionately patted House on the shoulder.

2.2 **D. 37**

Hank Aaron's power numbers increased as he aged. He posted four of his six 40-homer seasons after turning 30, and the most productive five-year home-run period of his career began at age 35. Aaron had his best total, 47 homers in 1971, at age 37. Part of the surge was a result of his move in 1966 from a very poor home-run park, County Stadium in Milwaukee, to a very good home-run park, Atlanta's Fulton County Stadium. But Aaron was also a biological marvel who retained his reflexes and hand-eye coordination until his forties. As well as belting 47 long flies in 1971, Aaron led the NL with a .669 slugging average, the best of any player during the era.

2.3 **A. Dick Allen of the White Sox**

One of baseball's most talented malcontents, Allen played for five different clubs, angering and frustrating teammates and managers with his indifferent work habits wherever he went. In 1974, the 32-year-old prompted more head shaking by announcing his retirement with 16 games left in the season, even though he was batting .301 and leading the AL in homers with 32. Allen's lead in the dinger derby held up, earning him the distinction of being the only player to win a home-run title while in retirement. Allen's departure proved short-lived. He returned in 1975 to play two more seasons with the Phillies and one with the A's, before hanging his spikes up for good after the 1977 campaign.

2.4 **A. Al Kaline**
Steadiness and longevity, two hallmarks of Kaline's career, helped him accomplish a remarkable statistical feat: amassing 399 career homers without hitting 30 homers in a season. Harold Baines is the only other player to top 300 dingers without a 30-homer campaign. Kaline would have reached the mark if he hadn't been plagued by injuries. In 1962, for example, one of the two years in which he hit 29 homers, Kaline had only 398 at-bats.

2.5 **B. He ranked among the AL's top ten in hits**
In 1980, George Brett waged a determined assault on the magical .400 barrier, last breached by Ted Williams in 1941. With two weeks left in the season, Brett was hitting exactly .400, but he tailed off and finished at .390. Still, it was the highest batting average by a third baseman in the 20th century. The Kansas City Royals star also drove in 118 runs in 117 games, the first time anyone had averaged more than an RBI per game since 1950, and his loop-leading .664 slugging average was the best in the AL since Mickey Mantle's .687 in 1961. As well, Brett hit 24 homers while fanning only 22 times. However, because he missed 45 games due to injuries, Brett collected only 175 hits, 15th best in the AL—an oddity for a player with such a lofty batting average.

2.6 **A. Reggie Jackson**
Oakland's big bopper was an alternate for the 1971 All-Star Game, picked by manager Earl Weaver to replace the injured Tony Oliva. Before leaving for the game, Jackson's teammate Sal Bando told him, "Don't embarrass us and strike out." Those words came back

George Brett: "He could get good wood on an aspirin."

to Jackson when he was sent in as a pinch-hitter in the third inning and promptly took two strikes from pitcher Dock Ellis. He choked up slightly on the bat and crushed Ellis's next offering, sending the ball rocketing upward, where it struck a light tower on the roof in right-center. Had the ball not hit the tower, it would have gone right out of Tiger Stadium. The mammoth blast earned Jackson his first dose of national TV exposure. It would not be the last.

2.7　B. Nate Colbert of the Padres

A good fastball hitter with a powerful, compact swing, Colbert was the San Diego Padres' only serious long-ball threat during the club's first few years of existence. In a doubleheader against the Atlanta Braves on August 1, 1972, he erupted for five homers, 13 RBI and 22 total bases. Colbert established a new record for the most RBI in a twinbill (tied by Mark Whiten in 1993) and equaled Stan Musial's mark for most homers in a doubleheader. Ironically, as an eight-year-old growing up in St. Louis, Colbert was at Sportsman's Park on May 2, 1954, to witness the doubleheader at which Musial had his five-homer outburst.

2.8　D. The 1987 Toronto Blue Jays

The power explosion occurred at Toronto's Exhibition Stadium on September 14, 1987, as the Blue Jays pulverized the Orioles 18–3. Ernie Whitt went yard three times, George Bell and Rance Mulliniks twice each, and Fred McGriff, Lloyd Moseby and Rob Ducey once. The previous record for most homers in a game was eight, a mark shared by several teams.

2.9　A. Jim Rice

Rice was so strong he once broke his bat on a checked swing *without* making contact with the ball. Yet, unlike some power hitters, there was also precision in Rice's swing. The Boston Red Sox slugger reached the 200-hit mark four times in his career, including three consecutive years from 1977 to 1979. In those three years he also hit 39, 46 and 39 homers, respectively. Rice was especially lethal in 1978, when he drilled an AL-high 213 hits and 46 homers and paced the loop with 15 triples, 139 rbi and 406 total bases, the most in the AL since Joe DiMaggio collected 418 total bases in 1937.

2.10   **A .204**

Dave Kingman was not much of a contact hitter, as attested by his career .236 batting average, but when he did make contact, the ball often traveled a long way. In 1982, the New York Mets first-sacker poled an NL-high 37 homers despite batting .204, by far the lowest batting average by a home-run champ. Kingman collected only 109 hits, but struck out 156 times.

LOWEST BATTING AVERAGES BY HOME-RUN CHAMPIONS*

Player	Year	League	Team	HR	Avg
Dave Kingman	1982	NL	Mets	37	.204
Harmon Killebrew	1959	AL	Senators	42	.242
Harmon Killebrew	1962	AL	Twins	48	.243
Gorman Thomas	1979	AL	Brewers	45	.244
Ralph Kiner	1952	NL	Pirates	37	.244
Gorman Thomas	1982	AL	Brewers	39	.245
Ralph Kiner	1946	NL	Pirates	23	.247

*CURRENT TO 1998

2.11   **C. Darrell Evans**

Until 1998, when Mark McGwire matched the feat, Evans was the only player to hit 40 homers in both leagues. In 1973, he drilled 41 four-baggers with the Atlanta Braves. Twelve years elapsed before Evans again reached the mark, this time with the Detroit Tigers in 1985, when he hit 40 on the nose.

2.12   **C. Mike Schmidt**

When the wind is blowing out at Wrigley Field, offensive fireworks are often the result. On April 17, 1976, aided by a 20 mile-per-hour breeze, Schmidt blasted four homers in four straight at-bats, including the game-winning two-run shot in the tenth inning. His fourth homer capped an eight-RBI, 5-for-6 day, as the Phillies outslugged the Cubs 18–16. Remarkably, Schmidt didn't hit his first homer until the fifth inning, with Philadelphia trailing 13–2.

2.13 A. Fred Lynn

NL manager Whitey Herzog instructed southpaw pitcher Atlee Hammaker to intentionally walk Robin Yount to get to the left-handed hitting Lynn in the third inning of the 1983 All-Star Game at Comiskey Park. The move backfired, as Lynn smashed a grand-slam homer into the right-field stands to key a seven-run uprising that sparked the AL to a 13–3 rout. The win ended an 11-game NL winning streak.

2.14 A. Hank Aaron

Hammerin' Hank cleared the fence 40 times in 392 at-bats in 1973, the most homers in history by a player with fewer than 400 at-bats. Although Aaron was an all-round hitting threat early in his career, as he zeroed in on Babe Ruth's career record for homers he became more of a long-ball specialist. A third of Aaron's hits in 1973 were four-baggers.

MOST HOMERS WITH LESS THAN 400 AT-BATS*

Player	Year	Team	AB	HR
Hank Aaron	1973	Braves	392	40
Mark McGwire	1995	Athletics	317	39
Frank Thomas	1994	White Sox	399	38
Barry Bonds	1994	Giants	391	37
Rudy York	1937	Tigers	375	35
Rob Deer	1992	Tigers	393	32
Mike Schmidt	1981	Phillies	354	31

* CURRENT TO 1998

2.15 C. Dave Kingman

Unless forced to retire because of injury, few hitters quit while they're still able to pound the ball out of the park. Yet Kingman could find no team interested in his services after 1986, a year in which the 37-year-old designated hitter thumped 35 homers and 94 RBI for the Oakland A's. Those are the best power numbers ever posted by a player in his final year. Kingman's surly personality and his toxic relations with the media helped to hasten his exit from baseball. In June 1986, he had a gift-wrapped live rat delivered to a female sportswriter for the *Sacramento Bee,* an incident that prompted the A's to fine him $3,500 and convinced the club not to renew his contract. Oakland replaced Kingman with 41-year-old Reggie Jackson, who produced 15 homers and 43 RBI in 1987.

MOST HOME RUNS IN FINAL YEAR*

Player	Year	Team	AB	HR
Dave Kingman	1986	Athletics	561	35
Ted Williams	1960	Red Sox	310	29
Hank Greenberg	1947	Pirates	402	25
Roy Cullenbine	1947	Tigers	464	24
Jack Graham	1949	Browns	500	24
Joe Gordon	1950	Indians	368	19

*CURRENT TO 1998

2.16 **D. 20**

Compared to the recent deluge of homers, the era between 1969 and 1989 appears to have been populated by 98-pound weaklings. Including the strike-shortened 1981 season, the home-run title was won by a player (or players) who hit less than 40 homers a total of 20 times. The power shortage was most acute in the AL in the mid-1970s, when three players won titles with just 32 round-trippers: Reggie Jackson (1973), Dick Allen (1974) and Graig Nettles (1976). In 1976, the second-place finisher in the AL home-run derby had 27 four-baggers, the equivalent of about two months' worth of Mark McGwire's output in 1998.

GAME 2

YOU CAN QUOTE ME

Shortly after joining the New York Yankees in 1977, Reggie Jackson gave a magazine interview, in which he said: "This team it all flows from me. I've got to keep it all going. I'm the straw that stirs the drink. Thurman Munson thinks he can be the straw that stirs the drink, but he can only stir it bad." Jackson's words certainly created a stir in the Yankee clubhouse. In particular, they created discord with Munson, the volatile Yankee captain. Inflammatory or not, the quote was pure Reggie. It's hard to imagine anyone else saying it. In this game, we ask you to match the baseball personality with his quote.

(Answers are on page 139)

Bill Lee	Bobby Bonds	George Brett	Graig Nettles
Yogi Berra	Bob Uecker	Billy Martin	Rickey Henderson
Pete Rose	Dick Allen	Gaylord Perry	Harmon Killebrew
Earl Weaver	Mickey Lolich	Reggie Jackson	Dan Quisenberry

1. "I'd walk through hell in a gasoline suit to keep playing baseball."

2. "When I was a little boy, I wanted to be a baseball player and join the circus. With the Yankees I've accomplished both."

3. "I once called the president of Vaseline and told him he should use me in a commercial since I use his product all the time. He got a little upset when he found out what I used it for. He said Vaseline is only for babies and fannies."

4. "I'll play first, third, left. I'll play anywhere—except Philadelphia."

GAME 2

5. "I would like to find a home in baseball. The only thing I've been a part of the last six years is American Airlines."

6. "All the fat guys look at me and say to their wives, 'See? There's a fat guy doing okay. Bring me another beer.'"

7. "I don't throw the first punch. I throw the second four."

8. "You can see a lot just by observing."

9. "It's what you learn after you know it all that counts."

10. "Most pitchers fear losing their fastball. Since I didn't have one, the only thing I fear is fear itself."

11. "Everybody tries to make hitting a science, which it is. But you can't treat it like a science; you have to treat it like an art."

12. "Anybody with ability can play in the big leagues. But to be able to trick people year in and year out, the way I did, I think that was a much greater feat."

13. "If my uniform doesn't get dirty, I haven't done anything in a game."

14. "I didn't have evil intentions, but I guess I did have power."

15. "I would never pitch for the Yankees because they represent everything that is wrong with America."

16. "I don't want to be a hero; I don't want to be a star. It just works out that way."

Nolan Ryan:
His smoking
fastball terrified
hitters for
27 seasons.

Chapter Three

FAST COMPANY

Nolan Ryan could really bring it. In 1974, his fastball was timed at 100.9 miles per hour. Traveling 56 feet from its point of release, the ball crossed the plate in 0.38 seconds. It's no wonder batters claimed that Ryan's heater appeared to explode into the strike zone. Yet even more impressive than his blinding speed was how long the Texan was able to maintain his velocity. During his 27-year career, Ryan notched 200 or more strikeouts 15 times. He topped 300 Ks on six occasions, the last time at age 42. On May 1, 1991, the 44-year-old added to his high-octane legend, fanning 16 batters and posting his seventh no-hitter. The team he blanked was the Toronto Blue Jays, the best-hitting club in the majors.   *(Answers are on page 36)*

3.1 **In 1986, Roger Clemens became the first pitcher to strike out 20 batters in a nine-inning game. Which team did he victimize in his milestone performance?**
A. The Texas Rangers
B. The Seattle Mariners
C. The Baltimore Orioles
D. The Milwaukee Brewers

3.2 **Sandy Koufax was the first NL southpaw to fan 300 batters in a season. Who was the first NL righty to reach the mark?**
A. Bob Gibson
B. Tom Seaver
C. Nolan Ryan
D. J.R. Richard

3.3 **Who started 49 games in 1972, the most by a pitcher since 1908?**
A. Mickey Lolich of the Tigers
B. Wilbur Wood of the White Sox
C. Ferguson Jenkins of the Cubs
D. Steve Carlton of the Phillies

3.4 **Which AL hurler pitched 22⅓ consecutive no-hit innings in 1977—the second-longest string in big-league annals?**
A. Luis Tiant of the Red Sox
B. Sparky Lyle of the Yankees
C. Frank Tanana of the Angels
D. Dennis Eckersley of the Indians

3.5 **Who gave pitcher Jim Hunter the nickname "Catfish"?**
A. His wife
B. His father
C. His club's owner
D. A sportswriter

3.6 **Who compiled a 21–20 record in 1979 to become the first hurler since 1881 to lead his league in both wins and losses?**
A. Phil Niekro of the Braves
B. Rick Reuschel of the Cubs
C. Jerry Koosman of the Twins
D. Ferguson Jenkins of the Rangers

3.7 **In what year did the save become an official pitching statistic?**
A. 1969
B. 1972
C. 1975
D. 1978

3.8 **Who posted the best winning percentage by a 20-game winner in major-league history?**

A. Ron Guidry of the Yankees

B. Roger Clemens of the Red Sox

C. David Cone of the Mets

D. Orel Hershiser of the Dodgers

3.9 **In 1974, who set a single-season mark for most decisions in relief, registering 17 wins and 14 losses out of the bullpen?**

A. Bill Campbell of the Twins

B. John Hiller of the Tigers

C. Gene Garber of the Phillies

D. Mike Marshall of the Dodgers

3.10 **Who is the only pitcher to fan 200 or more batters in nine straight seasons?**

A. Nolan Ryan

B. Tom Seaver

C. Bert Blyleven

D. Ferguson Jenkins

3.11 **What was known as "the pitch of the 1980s"?**

A. The slider

B. The screwball

C. The knuckleball

D. The split-fingered fastball

3.12 **Which relief ace was known as "the Australian"?**

A. Jeff Reardon

B. Bruce Sutter

C. Steve Bedrosian

D. Dan Quisenberry

3.13 **Which pennant winner boasted four 20-game winners?**

A. The 1971 Baltimore Orioles

B. The 1977 Los Angeles Dodgers

C. The 1986 New York Mets

D. The 1989 Oakland Athletics

3.14 **Who set the NL standard for most strikeouts in a season by a reliever?**
A. Bruce Sutter of the Cubs
B. Al Hrabosky of the Cardinals
C. Goose Gossage of the Pirates
D. Rollie Fingers of the Padres

3.15 **Who lost a league-high 20 games the year after he won the Cy Young Award?**
A. Randy Jones
B. Steve Carlton
C. Denny McLain
D. Gaylord Perry

3.16 **Which southpaw's career was saved when he underwent a revolutionary tendon transplant in his throwing arm in 1974?**
A. Jim Kaat
B. Jerry Reuss
C. Tommy John
D. Mickey Lolich

3.17 **Who set the all-time record for the lowest winning percentage by a league ERA leader?**
A. Mark Langston of the Mariners
B. Sam McDowell of the Indians
C. Nolan Ryan of the Astros
D. Jose DeLeon of the Cardinals

3.18 **Who matched Carl Hubbell's feat of striking out five straight batters in an All-Star Game?**
A. Jack Morris
B. Nolan Ryan
C. Mario Soto
D. Fernando Valenzuela

3.19 **What is pitcher Joe Cowley's claim to fame?**
A. He gave up Pete Rose's last hit
B. He won his first 12 major-league decisions
C. He is the last AL pitcher to steal home
D. His last win in the majors was a no-hitter

3.20 **Which lefty twirled ten shutouts in 1985, one shy of the all-time mark for southpaws?**
A. Ron Guidry
B. Frank Viola
C. John Tudor
D. Fernando Valenzuela

3.21 **Which pitcher threatened to sue an umpire for interfering with his ability to make a living, after he was ejected from a game for doctoring the baseball?**
A. Don Sutton of the Dodgers
B. Joe Niekro of the Astros
C. Mike Flanagan of the Orioles
D. Rick Honeycutt of the Mariners

3.22 **Which pitcher's career came to a premature end when he developed a mental block about throwing strikes?**
A. Burt Hooton
B. Steve Blass
C. Pascual Perez
D. Mark Fidrych

3.23 **In 1988, which pitcher was denied no-hitters in back-to-back games by allowing a two-out base hit in the ninth inning?**
A. Tom Browning of the Reds
B. Greg Maddux of the Cubs
C. Dave Stieb of the Blue Jays
D. Bret Saberhagen of the Royals

Answers

FAST COMPANY

3.1   B. The Seattle Mariners

After Roger Clemens underwent shoulder surgery in August 1985, some doubted the 23-year-old would be able recapture his awesome velocity. Clemens supplied his answer early in the 1986 campaign. On a chilly night at Fenway Park on April 29, the Red Sox ace blew away the Seattle Mariners, fanning 20 batters with a fastball clocked at 98 miles per hour. The Rocket Man allowed only three hits and no walks in the 3–1 win. Clemens struck out every Mariner at least once and whiffed Phil Bradley four times, the last time with one out in the ninth to nail down the record. The victory was, coincidentally, the 20th of Clemens's career.

3.2   D. J.R. Richard

If his career had not been derailed by a stroke in 1980, there is no telling what Richard might have accomplished. At six feet eight inches, the towering Astros hurler was not only baseball's tallest pitcher but perhaps its hardest thrower. His buzzing fastball was especially intimidating because Richard's control was always an iffy thing. Teammate Bob Watson admitted: "I've never taken batting practice against him and I never will. I have a family to think about." In 1978, Richard struck out 303 batters to become the first right-hander in NL history to reach the milestone. In 1979, he extended his record by fanning 313.

3.3   B. Wilbur Wood of the White Sox

Wood's middle name should have been workhorse. In 1968, the knuckleballer appeared in a record 88 games as a reliever for the

Chicago White Sox. Five years later, in 1972, he started an amazing 49 games for the Pale Hose, pitching 376 ⅔ innings, with a 24–17 won–lost record and a 2.51 ERA. Only one other 20th-century pitcher—Jack Chesbro, with 51 in 1904—started more games in a season. Wood's resilient arm was evidently unaffected by the toil. The next season he started 48 games and won 24 again. In fact, in a five-year span from 1971 to 1975, Wood started 224 games for Chicago—an average of 45 starts per year.

3.4   D. Dennis Eckersley of the Indians

Eckersley was within six outs of equalling Cy Young's 1904 record of 24 ⅓ consecutive no-hit innings, when he gave up a two-out homer to Seattle's Ruppert Jones in the sixth inning of a game on June 5, 1977. In his two previous starts, Eckersley had pitched a nine-inning no-hitter against the Angels and seven and two-thirds hitless innings against the Mariners.

3.5   C. His club's owner

Charlie Finley signed pitcher James Augustus Hunter upon his graduation from high school in 1964. To hype the signing, the A's owner decided that Hunter needed a nickname. Since the teenager liked to hunt and fish and because he hailed from a small town in North Carolina, Finley told the youngster that he was going to be known as Catfish. Finley even concocted a tale set in Hunter's childhood to explain how he had acquired the countrified nickname. Much to the chagrin of Hunter's parents, the moniker stuck, and with Hunter's rise to fame it became one of the celebrated nicknames in baseball history.

3.6   A. Phil Niekro of the Braves

In 1979, the knuckleball artist topped the NL with 21 wins, but he also led the loop in losses with 20, a rare feat. Clearly, playing for Atlanta was a factor: the Braves placed last in the NL West with a 66–94 record. Niekro's capacity for work also figured in the equation: he logged 342 innings and got decisions in 41 of the 44 games in which he pitched. The last hurler before Niekro to lead his league in both categories was Boston's Jim Whitney in 1881, and Whitney started 63 of his team's 83 games.

3.7 **A. 1969**

The save became an officially recognized statistic in 1969, and relief pitchers and their agents are eternally grateful. Awarded to relievers who protected leads in their team's victories, the stat helped raise the profile and earning power of late-inning stoppers. The Dodgers' Bill Singer became the first pitcher credited with a save, when he relieved Don Drysdale in the season-opener at Cincinnati on April 7 and pitched three scoreless innings to preserve a 3–2 win.

3.8 **A. Ron Guidry of the Yankees**

They began calling Ron Guidry "Louisiana Lightning" in 1978. It was an apt moniker, as few pitchers have had a more electrifying season. The Yankee lefty went 25–3, with a 1.74 ERA, 248 strikeouts and nine shutouts. His .893 winning percentage was the best of any 20-game winner in history. New York's record in Guidry's 35 starts was 30–5. The southpaw's sensational pitching was the main reason the Yankees were able to overtake the Boston Red Sox after trailing in the AL East by 14 games in July. Oddly, all three of Guidry's losses in 1978 were to left-handed pitchers named Mike: Mike Flanagan, Mike Caldwell and Mike Willis.

HIGHEST WINNING-PERCENTAGE (20 WINS OR MORE)*

Pitcher	Year	Team	W–L	Pct
Ron Guidry	1978	Yankees	25–3	.893
Lefty Grove	1931	Athletics	31–4	.886
Preacher Roe	1951	Dodgers	22–3	.880
Joe Wood	1912	Red Sox	34–5	.872
David Cone	1988	Mets	20–3	.870
Bill Donovan	1907	Tigers	25–4	.862
Whitey Ford	1961	Yankees	25–4	.862
Dwight Gooden	1985	Mets	24–4	.857
Roger Clemens	1986	Red Sox	24–4	.857

*CURRENT TO 1998

3.9   B. John Hiller of the Tigers

Hiller racked up an eye-popping 17–14 record with the Detroit Tigers in 1974 to set a record for most decisions by a reliever. It's a doubly amazing achievement, considering the circumstances. Three years before, Hiller's life was in jeopardy after he suffered a massive stroke. But the Canadian southpaw made a miraculous recovery and was pitching batting practice by the end of 1972. In 1973, he dispelled any lingering concerns about his health by turning in a superb season, appearing in an AL-high 65 games, with a 10–5 record, 38 saves and a 1.44 ERA.

3.10   B. Tom Seaver

The rifle-armed righty topped the 200-strikeout plateau nine straight years between 1968 and 1976, and came very close to doing it 11 years in a row. In 1977, Seaver fell just four K's short of the mark, before rebounding in 1978 to fan 226. Although Nolan Ryan might seem the logical choice for this record, Ryan's longest consecutive string of 200-strikeout seasons was five.

3.11   D. The split-fingered fastball

The pitch is thrown with the same arm motion as a fastball, but it is released from between split fingers, rather than off the fingertips, which slows its speed. When thrown properly, it tends to dive straight down as it reaches the plate, making it tough to hit. Reliever Bruce Sutter, in the late 1970s, was the first hurler to ride the splitter to fame, but the pitch reached its peak of popularity in the mid-1980s, when Mike Scott and Jack Morris were its most celebrated practitioners. Roger Craig, the split-fingered guru, had his staff in San Francisco use it so extensively in the 1980s that it was said that the SF on the players' caps actually stood for split-fingered.

3.12   D. Dan Quisenberry

The Kansas City Royals closer was called "the Australian" because of his sweeping sidearm delivery—in other words, pitching from "down under." Quisenberry led the AL in saves five times in six years from 1980 to 1985, including back-to-back seasons of 45 and 44 saves. In addition to a first-rate sinkerball, Quisenberry also had a quirky sense of humor. Commenting on his success, he said, "I broke my slump when I found a delivery in my flaw." Another time, describing the job of a relief pitcher, Quisenberry observed, "We're parasites. We live off the people who spend two hours on the field."

3.13 A. The 1971 Baltimore Orioles

A stunning 81 of the Orioles' 101 wins in 1971 came courtesy of four strong-armed starters: Dave McNally (21–5), Mike Cueller (20–9), Jim Palmer (20–9) and Pat Dobson (20–8). Only one other team in big-league history—the 1920 Chicago White Sox—has ever had four 20-game winners. Yet, even with their four aces, the Orioles failed to win the World Series, losing in seven games to the Pittsburgh Pirates, a team without a single 20-game winner.

3.14 C. Goose Gossage of the Pirates

Gossage spent only one year with Pittsburgh, but he made quite an impact, notching an 11–9 record with 26 saves and a 1.62 ERA in 1977. The fireballer also fanned 151 batters in 133 innings to break Mike Marshall's NL mark for most strikeouts by a reliever. In 1978, Gossage signed as a free agent with the New York Yankees, where he would become the junior circuit's dominant closer.

3.15 B. Steve Carlton

Carlton was an overpowering force in 1972, leading in the NL in wins (27) strikeouts (310) and ERA (1.97) with the last-place Philadelphia Phillies. His dominance on the mound was reflected in the Cy Young Award voting, where he garnered all 24 first-place votes. There was no way Carlton could have matched that Herculean effort in 1973, but the drop in his production was startling. Although the Phillies won 12 more games than they had in 1972, Carlton lost an NL-high 20 games, while winning just 13, and saw his ERA balloon to 3.90.

3.16 C. Tommy John

The 12-year veteran ruptured a ligament in his pitching arm during a game against the Montreal Expos on July 17, 1974. In a bid to save his career, he underwent an experimental surgical procedure that involved transplanting a tendon from his right wrist into his damaged left arm. After missing all of 1975, John returned in 1976 to

Goose Gossage: He closed games with a scowl and a high-90s hummer.

post a 10–10 record and win the award for Comeback Player of the Year. Although he was never a speedballer, John's velocity was even less after the surgery, which prompted him to joke, "When they operated I told them to put in a Koufax fastball. They did—but it was Mrs. Koufax's." But John persevered, carving out a stellar career by relying on guile and finesse. Equipped with his "bionic" arm, he would pitch 26 seasons and amass 288 career victories.

3.17   C. Nolan Ryan of the Astros

Here's a case for Sherlock Holmes. In 1987, Ryan led the NL with 270 strikeouts and a 2.76 ERA and allowed only 6.55 hits per nine innings, easily the best ratio in the league. Yet, somehow, the flamethrower posted an anemic 8–16 won–lost record. His .333 winning percentage constitutes an all-time low for an ERA champ. It's true that Houston did not have a strong hitting team (only the Dodgers scored fewer runs), but even so, four of Ryan's teammates managed to win more games than he did and all had much higher ERAs. Mike Scott won 16 games, double Ryan's production.

LOWEST WINNING-PERCENTAGE BY AN ERA LEADER*

Pitcher	Year	Team	IP	ERA	W–L	Pct
Nolan Ryan	1987	Astros	211	2.76	8–16	.333
Joe Magrane	1988	Cardinals	165	2.18	5–9	.357
Rube Waddell	1900	Pirates	208	2.37	8–13	.381
Stu Miller	1958	Giants	182	2.47	6–9	.400
Ed Siever	1902	Tigers	188	1.91	8–11	.421
Dave Koslo	1949	Giants	212	2.50	11–14	.440
Dolf Luque	1924	Reds	291	2.63	16–18	.471

*CURRENT TO 1998

3.18   D. Fernando Valenzuela

During the fourth inning of the 1986 All-Star Game at Houston's Astrodome, the Dodger lefty struck out, in order, Don Mattingly, Cal Ripken and Jesse Barfield. In the fifth, he fanned Lou Whitaker and Teddy Higuera, before Kirby Puckett ended the humiliation by grounding out. Valenzuela had tied the All-Star Game record for consecutive strikeouts, set 52 years earlier by Carl Hubbell of the New York Giants. Like Valenzuela, Hubbell was also a screwball specialist, but the hitters that he disposed of—Babe Ruth, Lou Gehrig, Jimmie Foxx, Al Simmons and Joe Cronin— were of higher caliber.

3.19   D. His last win in the majors was a no-hitter

On September 19, 1986, Chicago White Sox hurler Joe Cowley twirled a no-hitter, beating the California Angels 7-1 to even his season's mark at 11-11. Cowley was traded to Philadelphia after the season, where he pitched abysmally, losing four games and posting a 15.43 ERA in 11 ⅔ innings. The Phillies sent Cowley to the minors. He never made it back to the bigs, thereby becoming the only pitcher whose last win was a no-hitter.

3.20   C. John Tudor

In his first six years in the majors, Tudor had never won more than 13 games or posted an ERA under 3.00, and had only four shutouts to his credit. So his superb 1975 performance with the St. Louis Cardinals came as a major surprise. After a sputtering start, the crafty lefty won 20 of his last 21 decisions, to finish with a 21–8 record, a 1.93 ERA and 10 shutouts. Only one other southpaw has ever recorded more goose eggs: Sandy Koufax, with 11 in 1963.

3.21   A. Don Sutton of the Dodgers

Umpire Doug Harvey gave Sutton the heave during a game on July 14, 1978, after he collected three balls that had become mysteriously defaced while in Sutton's hands. Fearing that he would be suspended, the Dodger pitcher threatened to sue Harvey for jeopardizing his ability to earn a living. NL president Chub Feeney let Sutton off with a warning, but no suspension. Sutton was so often accused of ball tampering that he eventually developed a sense of humor about his reputation. One umpire who came out to the mound to search Sutton for suspicious objects discovered a note inside the pitcher's glove. It read: "You're getting warm, but it's not there." Whatever Sutton was doing to the ball, it obviously worked. He posted 324 wins in his 23-year career.

3.22 **B. Steve Blass**

Renowned for his pinpoint control, the veteran ace of the Pirates' staff enjoyed a fine season in 1972, when he went 19–8 with a 2.49 ERA. But the following year, the 31-year-old suddenly lost his ability to get the ball over the plate. Blass tried Transcendental Meditation, psychotherapy and hypnosis in an attempt to solve the problem, but nothing helped. After 1972, he won only three more games. In his last spring training with the Pirates in 1974, Blass pitched 20 innings, allowing 17 hits, 33 walks and 22 runs, while hitting 10 batters. He told reporters, "You have no idea how frustrating it is. You don't know where you're going to throw the ball. You know you're embarrassing yourself, but you can't do anything about it. You're totally afraid and helpless." Today, pitchers who develop this subconscious fear are said to suffer from "Steve Blass disease."

3.23 **C. Dave Stieb of the Blue Jays**

In September 1988, the Blue Jays mainstay lost no-hitters in back-to-back starts, both times by allowing hits with two outs in the ninth inning. Incredibly, in his second start in 1989, Stieb pitched another one-hitter, becoming the first pitcher to throw three one-hitters in four starts. He would pitch another one-hitter during 1989, his fourth in less than a year. On August 4, 1989, the hard-luck hurler suffered more frustration, losing a perfect game by the slimmest of margins, when Roberto Kelly of the Yankees doubled with two outs in the ninth. Steve Sax then singled to drive home Kelly, and Stieb had to settle for a two-hitter and a 2–1 victory. Stieb finally ended his exasperating quest for perfection by no-hitting the Cleveland Indians 3–0 in 1990.

MOUND MAGICIANS

The 1970s and 1980s were aglitter with superb pitching performances. Match the hurler with his accomplishment. *(Answers are on page 139)*

Tom Seaver	Jim Palmer	Gaylord Perry	Bill Gullickson
Jim Kaat	Randy Jones	Don Sutton	Catfish Hunter
Nolan Ryan	Phil Niekro	Steve Carlton	Ferguson Jenkins

1. _____ Tossed two no-hitters in one season.

2. _____ Led his league in innings pitched four times.

3. _____ Won 16 Gold Glove Awards.

4. _____ Pitched a perfect game.

5. _____ Notched ten shutouts in a season.

6. _____ Captured four Cy Young Awards.

7. _____ Posted six straight 20-win seasons.

8. _____ First pitcher to notch 100 Ks in 20 straight seasons.

9. _____ Had a record 16 Opening-Day starts.

10. _____ Was the first rookie to fan 18 batters in a game.

11. _____ Did not allow a walk in 68 straight innings.

12. _____ Won the Cy Young Award in both the AL and NL.

Roberto Clemente: He claimed four batting titles and 12 Gold Gloves.

Chapter Four

BY THE NUMBERS

Some baseball numbers possess a special magic: 300 wins, 500 homers, 3,000 hits. In the case of Roberto Clemente, 3,000 hits has an added resonance. The Pirates star reached the milestone on September 30, 1972, doubling off Mets pitcher Jon Matlack in his last at-bat of the season. As it turned out, it was also the last regular-season hit of his career. In December an earthquake devastated Nicaragua, and Clemente volunteered to help deliver relief supplies to the victims. His plane crashed into the Atlantic Ocean just after takeoff on New Year's Eve, killing all on board. In tribute, the Hall of Fame waived its customary five-year waiting period and inducted Clemente into Cooperstown 11 weeks later.

In this chapter, we look at some other notable baseball numbers.

(Answers are on page 51)

4.1 **In 1978, Pete Rose equaled an 81-year-old NL record by hitting safely in how many straight games?**

A. 36

B. 40

C. 44

D. 48

4.2 **Whose number was *not* retired by two different teams?**
A. Rod Carew's
B. Hank Aaron's
C. Rollie Fingers's
D. Reggie Jackson's

4.3 **How many times did Billy Martin manage the New York Yankees?**
A. Three times
B. Four times
C. Five times
D. Six times

4.4 **The Montreal Expos joined the National League in 1969. How much time elapsed before an Expos pitcher tossed a no-hitter?**
A. Nine days
B. Nine weeks
C. Nine months
D. Nine years

4.5 **Which is the higher number?**
A. Career wins by Ron Guidry
B. Complete games pitched by Don Sutton
C. Most strikeouts in a season by Catfish Hunter
D. Double-digit strikeout games by Nolan Ryan

4.6 **Phil Niekro won 318 games in his career. How many wins did Niekro have before he turned 30 years of age?**
A. 31
B. 81
C. 131
D. 181

4.7 **The number seven had a special significance for pitcher Dock Ellis in 1977. Why?**
A. He was ejected from seven games
B. He played for seven different managers
C. He got married for the seventh time
D. He stole seven bases, a record for pitchers

4.8 In 1982, Rickey Henderson set a major-league record for most stolen bases in a season. How many did he steal?

A. 110

B. 120

C. 130

D. 140

4.9 In 1973, the American League introduced the designated hitter. Many predicted AL pitching would suffer as a result. How many 20-game winners were there in the two leagues that year?

A. One in the AL, 12 in the NL

B. Four in the AL, eight in the NL

C. Six in the AL, six in the NL

D. 12 in the AL, one in the NL

4.10 Who is the only batting champion since 1901 to post an average 50 points higher than any other player in his league?

A. Wade Boggs

B. Rod Carew

C. Tony Gwynn

D. George Brett

4.11 Orel Hershiser of the Dodgers set a major-league record by pitching how many consecutive scoreless innings in 1988?

A. 49

B. 54

C. 59

D. 64

4.12 Which number is *not* zero?

A. Games started by Rollie Fingers

B. Inside-the-park homers hit by Frank Robinson

C. Seasons that Willie Mays led the NL in RBI

D. Grand-slam homers allowed by Jim Palmer

4.13 How often did Reggie Jackson strike out during his career?
A. 1,597 times
B. 2,097 times
C. 2,597 times
D. 3,097 times

4.14 Which two players ended their careers with exactly the same number of RBI?
A. Joe Morgan and Pete Rose
B. George Brett and Mike Schmidt
C. Roberto Clemente and Andre Dawson
D. Reggie Jackson and Dave Winfield

4.15 In what year did the Chicago Cubs play their first night game at Wrigley Field?
A. 1979
B. 1982
C. 1985
D. 1988

4.16 Since 1920, what is the record for the most losses in a season by a pitcher with an ERA below 2.00?
A. 10
B. 13
C. 16
D. 19

4.17 Which pitcher asked to have his uniform number changed from 37 to 337 before the start of the 1973 season, and why?
A. Bob Moose of the Pirates
B. Mike Marshall of the Expos
C. Bill Lee of the Red Sox
D. Blue Moon Odom of the Athletics

BY THE NUMBERS

4.1   **C. 44**

On June 14, 1978, Pete Rose broke out of a 5-for-44 batting slump with two hits against the Chicago Cubs. For the next six weeks, no pitcher was able to keep Rose off base, as he continued delivering line-drive hits. Six times he preserved the streak with his last at-bat; in four games his only hit was a bunt. The streak finally ended on August 1, when Rose went hitless in five plate appearances against Braves pitchers Larry McWilliams and Gene Garber. During his record 44-game run, he batted .385 with 70 hits. Rose tied Willie Keeler's NL mark for most consecutive games with a hit, and was only 12 games short of Joe DiMaggio's all-time record of 56 games.

4.2   **D. Reggie Jackson's**

Jackson's number 44 has only been retired by one team: the New York Yankees. Rod Carew's number 29 was retired by the Minnesota Twins and the California Angels, Hank Aaron's number 44 by the Atlanta Braves and Milwaukee Brewers, and Rollie Fingers's number 34 by the Oakland A's and Milwaukee Brewers.

4.3   **C. Five times**

Trigger-happy Yankees owner George Steinbrenner hired and fired Billy Martin five times during a span of 14 years from 1975 to 1988, even though Martin never had a losing season. It's conceivable that Steinbrenner might have brought the combative skipper back to manage the Yankees for a sixth time, if Martin had not been killed in a car crash in 1989.

4.4 A. Nine days

The Expos' Bill Stoneman no-hit the Phillies 7–0 at Connie Mack Stadium on April 17, 1969, only nine days after Montreal played its first game in the majors. It marked the first time that a pitcher on an expansion team had tossed a no-hitter in his club's inaugural season. On October 2, 1972, at Montreal's Jarry Park, Stoneman tossed the second no-hitter by an Expo and the first by a major leaguer in Canada, blanking the Mets 7–0.

4.5 D. Double-digit strikeout games by Nolan Ryan

Among Ryan's catalog of strikeout feats, this one stands out. The fireballer fanned ten or more batters in a mind-boggling 215 games. Second in the category is Sandy Koufax, who turned the trick 97 times. Steve Carlton is third at 83. Even if we combined the totals of those two Hall of Famers, they would still be 35 games behind Ryan. As for the other options in the question: Catfish Hunter's top strikeout total was 196; Don Sutton pitched 178 complete games; and Ron Guidry had 170 career wins.

4.6 A. 31

Phil Niekro's career did not conform to conventional timelines. The knuckleballer, who began his career as a reliever, did not post his first win until 1965, when he was 26, and he had only 31 victories before the age of 30, by far the fewest of any 300-game winner. In contrast, Catfish Hunter, who was seven years younger than Niekro and who also won his first game in 1965, had 184 wins by age 30. Hunter went on to accumulate 224 wins, while Niekro would get 318, evidence of how productive he was in his later years. In fact, the knuckleballer did not surpass the 200-win mark until after turning 40.

4.7 B. He played for seven different managers

Dock Ellis experienced plenty of changes in 1977. After starting three games for the New York Yankees and manager Billy Martin in April, he was traded to the Oakland A's. In June, a week after A's manager Jack McKeon was fired and replaced by Bobby Winkles, Ellis was traded again, this time to the Texas Rangers. A week after Ellis's arrival, the Rangers axed manager Frank Lucchesi. His replacement, Eddie Stanky, quit after one game. Third-base coach Connie Ryan managed the club for six games, until Billy Hunter was hired, upping the number of field bosses that Ellis had played for to seven—the most by any player in one season.

4.8   **C. 130**

In describing Rickey Henderson, pitcher Doc Medich said, "He's like a little kid in a train station. You turn your back on him and he's gone." In 1982, Rickey Henderson was gone more often than any player in history. The "Man of Steal" swiped 130 bases in 149 games to shatter Lou Brock's record of 118. No one has come close to the mark since, just as no player is likely to challenge Henderson's career stolen-base total, which had reached 1,297 by the end of 1998.

MOST STOLEN BASES IN A SEASON*

Player	Year	Team	SB	CS	Pct
Rickey Henderson	1982	Athletics	130	42	.76
Lou Brock	1974	Cardinals	118	33	.78
Vince Coleman	1985	Cardinals	110	25	.81
Vince Coleman	1987	Cardinals	109	22	.83
Rickey Henderson	1983	Athletics	108	19	.85
Vince Coleman	1986	Cardinals	107	14	.88
Maury Wills	1962	Dodgers	104	13	.89
Rickey Henderson	1980	Athletics	100	26	.79

*CURRENT TO 1998

4.9   **D. 12 in the AL, one in the NL**

As expected, the introduction of the designated hitter in 1973 did boost AL hitting. The loop's overall batting average rose to .259 from .239, and homers jumped from 1,175 to 1,552. But the DH also had a positive effect on pitchers' win totals. No fewer than 12 AL pitchers won 20 games, compared with one in the NL. In 1972, only six AL pitchers had reached the mark. Because of the DH, AL managers tended to leave their starting pitchers in games longer, thus improving their chances for decisions. As a result, the number of complete games pitched in the AL in 1973 rose to 614 from 502 in 1972. The pattern continued in 1974, as nine AL pitchers reached the 20-win plateau, compared with two in the NL.

4.10 B. Rod Carew

An opponent once described Carew as the "only player I know who can go 4-for-3." A spray hitter who studied pitchers and adjusted his batting stance to combat their strengths, the Panamanian batted over .300 in 15 seasons. He won seven batting titles, the most impressive in 1977, when he hit .388 for the Minnesota Twins. That figure was .052 percentage points higher than runner-up Lyman Bostock, the largest victory margin by a batting champion since Nap Lajoie in 1901.

LARGEST MARGIN OF VICTORY BY BATTING CHAMPIONS*

Year	Team	Leader and runner-up	Avg	Margin
1901	Athletics	Nap Lajoie	.426	.086
	Orioles	Mike Donlin	.340	
1977	Twins	Rod Carew	.388	.052
	Twins	Lyman Bostock	.336	
1924	Cardinals	Rogers Hornsby	.424	.049
	Dodgers	Zach Wheat	.375	
1974	Twins	Rod Carew	.364	.048
	White Sox	Jorge Orta	.316	
1941	Red Sox	Ted Williams	.406	.047
	Senators	Cecil Travis	.359	
1922	Cardinals	Rogers Hornsby	.401	.047
	Cubs	Ray Grimes	.354	
1921	Cardinals	Rogers Hornsby	.397	.047
	Cardinals	Austin McHenry	.350	

*1901 TO 1998

4.11 C. 59

Orel Hershiser was in a zone during the last month of 1988: the zero zone. After tossing four scoreless innings against the Expos on August 30, 1988, the Dodger righty reeled off five straight shut-

Rod Carew: He batted over .300 for 15 consecutive seasons.

outs—a total of 49 blank frames. That left him nine and two-thirds innings short of Don Drysdale's 1968 record of 58⅔ consecutive scoreless innings. Since Hershiser had only one start left in the season, the record seemed out of reach. But on September 28, Hershiser and the Padres' Andy Hawkins hooked up in a nine-inning shutout duel. When Hershiser blanked the Padres in the tenth, he eclipsed Drysdale's mark. Manager Tommy Lasorda then removed Hershiser from the game to save his arm for the playoffs.

Incredibly, he tossed eight more scoreless frames against the Mets in his first start in the NLCS, but because those innings came in the postseason they were not included in his streak.

4.12   A. Games started by Rollie Fingers

Fingers may have made his name by coming out of the bullpen, but he also started 37 games early in his career for the Oakland A's, going the distance four times. Surprisingly, all the other options in the question are zeroes. Willie Mays never led his league in runs batted in during his 22-year career, none of Frank Robinson's 586 homers were inside-the-park jobs and Jim Palmer did not allow a grand slam in 3,948 innings.

4.13   C. 2,597 times

People loved to watch Reggie Jackson play for one of two reasons: to see him hit homers or to see him strike out. Jackson performed both tasks with distinctive flair, but his whiffs were far more frequent. He amassed a major-league record 2,597 strikeouts, 661 more than his nearest rival, Willie Stargell. If you prorate Jackson's strikeout total at 500 at-bats per year, it means that in five of his 21 seasons, Jackson never touched the ball.

4.14   B. George Brett and Mike Schmidt

It's a nice irony that the top two third-basemen of their day should both conclude their careers with 1,595 RBI. Considering Schmidt's decided edge in power, you might expect him to lead in the category. Schmidt hit 213 more homers than Brett and had nine 100-RBI seasons, compared with Brett's four. But the Royals star was a consistent run producer and had 1,997 more at-bats than Schmidt.

4.15   D. 1988

Although every other major-league team had lights by 1948, the Chicago Cubs stubbornly stuck to a policy of daylight games only until August 8, 1988, when Wrigley Field finally hosted its first night game. Not everyone welcomed the development. Said sportswriter Roger Simon: "Putting lights in Wrigley Field is like putting aluminum siding on the Sistine Chapel." The baseball gods seemed to agree with Simon. A violent thunderstorm caused the historic game with the Phillies to be canceled after only three innings. As a result, the park's first official night game was played the next night against the Mets. The Cubs won 6–4.

4.16 C. 16

One wonders how many games Gaylord Perry might have won in 1972 if he had been pitching for a contender instead of the fifth-place Cleveland Indians. As it was, Perry still won an AL-high 24 games and posted a sparkling 1.92 ERA. He earned decisions in all 40 games he started and made one relief appearance as well. Perry copped the 1972 Cy Young Award for his yeoman duty, despite losing 16 games. Not only is that the most losses by any Cy Young recipient, you have to go all the way back to 1918 to find a pitcher who lost as many games with an ERA under 2.00.

MOST LOSSES WITH AN ERA UNDER 2.00*

Pitcher	Year	Team	W	L	ERA
Gaylord Perry	1972	Indians	24	16	1.92
Sam McDowell	1968	Indians	15	14	1.81
Wilbur Wood	1971	White Sox	22	13	1.91
Carl Hubbell	1933	Giants	23	12	1.66
Kevin Brown	1996	Marlins	17	11	1.89

*1920 TO 1998

4.17 C. Bill Lee of the Red Sox

Loved by fans because he was different and by sportswriters because was so quotable, the eccentric southpaw was always ruffling the feathers of Boston's conservative management. Lee staged a one-day strike in 1978, when the Red Sox sold his friend Bernie Carbo to Cleveland. The team responded by fining him a day's pay. Lee asked if they would triple the fine and give him the weekend off. It's hard to say if Lee was serious in his request for number 337, because he was turned down. When asked why he wanted the unwieldy number, the Spaceman explained, "Because if you turn 337 upside down it spells LEE. And then I could stand on my head and people would know me right away."

HIGHER OR LOWER?

Ballplayers say that a key to winning games is maintaining emotional control—not allowing yourself to get too high or too low. Unfortunately, that strategy won't work in this game—you have to go high. Select the larger number for each of the options below. Count five points for each A answer and ten points for each B answer. If you've answered each one correctly, the total of your responses will supply the mystery number at the bottom of the next page.

(Answers are on page 139)

1. A. Seasons played by Brooks Robinson.

    B. Seasons played by Frank Robinson.

2. A. Lou Brock's career strikeout total.

    B. Hank Aaron's career strikeout total.

3. A. Highest RBI season by Don Mattingly.

    B. Highest RBI season by Mike Schmidt.

4. A. Career homers hit by Dwight Evans

    B. Career homers hit by Darrell Evans.

5. A. Years that Joe Morgan spent with Houston.

    B. Years that Joe Morgan spent with Cincinnati.

6. A. Johnny Bench's career batting average.

    B. Thurman Munson's career batting average.

7. A. Times that Joe Niekro led his league in losses.

    B. Times that Phil Niekro led his league in losses.

8. A. Batting titles won by Pete Rose.

    B. Batting titles won by Bill Madlock.

9. A. Age at which Robin Yount debuted in the majors.

    B. Age at which Paul Molitor debuted in the majors.

10. A. Complete games pitched by Bert Blyleven.

    B. Complete games pitched by Nolan Ryan.

MYSTERY NUMBER:
Willie Stargell's career total of sacrifice flies _____

Willie McCovey: When he connected, the ball left the park in a hurry.

Chapter Five

THE RECORD REALM

Willie McCovey's swing was a thing of deadly beauty. Balls jumped off his bat like rocket-powered missiles. When he took one of his mighty left-handed cuts, the lanky six-foot-four slugger looked as though he was covering everything, in the words of one pitcher, "from the inside corner to halfway up the third-base line." Wary pitchers issued McCovey 260 intentional walks in his career, including a major-league record 45 in 1969. Despite all the free passes, "Stretch" still got his licks in. He led the league in homers (45), RBI (126) and slugging average (.659) and won the MVP Award. When McCovey retired in 1980, he had clouted 521 homers and an NL-record 18 grand slams. Opposition pitchers were not sad to see him go. Said Dodger Don Sutton: "He was easily the most feared hitter in the league. He was awesome." *(Answers are on page 65)*

5.1 **Which player banged his way into the record books by collecting five hits in back-to-back games in 1970?**
A. Tony Oliva of the Twins
B. Reggie Smith of the Red Sox
C. Willie Davis of the Dodgers
D. Roberto Clemente of the Pirates

5.2 **Who logged a record seven straight 200-hit seasons?**
A. Rod Carew
B. Wade Boggs
C. Pete Rose
D. Tony Gwynn

5.3 **Which third baseman set the all-time highs for most putouts and most double plays in a season?**
A. Mike Schmidt
B. Graig Nettles
C. Buddy Bell
D. Brooks Robinson

5.4 **Who is the only pitcher to strike out ten batters in a row?**
A. Roger Clemens
B. Tom Seaver
C. Steve Carlton
D. Sam McDowell

5.5 **What 20th-century record did the Pirates' Rennie Stennett set in a nine-inning game in 1975?**
A. He scored six runs
B. He stole home twice
C. He collected seven hits
D. He had nine at-bats

5.6 **Who established a milestone in 1972 by driving in the highest percentage of a team's runs in big-league history?**
A. Dick Allen of the White Sox
B. Frank Howard of the Senators
C. Billy Williams of the Cubs
D. Nate Colbert of the Padres

5.7 **Who holds the mark for the most RBI in a season by a full-time designated hitter?**
A. Don Baylor of the Angels
B. Hal McRae of the Royals

C. Andre Thornton of the Indians

D. Greg Luzinski of the White Sox

5.8 **Who holds the record for most Gold Glove Awards by a second baseman?**

A. Frank White

B. Bobby Grich

C. Joe Morgan

D. Ryne Sandberg

5.9 **Who struck out a record 189 times in a single season?**

A. Rob Deer

B. Bobby Bonds

C. Mike Schmidt

D. Jose Canseco

5.10 **Which rubber-armed reliever set a major-league record by appearing in 106 games in one season?**

A. Wayne Granger of the Reds

B. Dick Tidrow of the Cubs

C. Kent Tekulve of the Pirates

D. Mike Marshall of the Dodgers

5.11 **Which record did pitcher Jim Barr set with the San Francisco Giants in 1972?**

A. He retired 41 batters in a row

B. He lost his first 15 decisions

C. He uncorked six wild pitches in one game

D. He pitched three consecutive one-hitters

5.12 **How old was Lou Brock when he set a major-league record by stealing 118 bases in a season?**

A. 26

B. 29

C. 32

D. 35

5.13 **Who does *not* hold the record for career homers for his position?**
A. Hank Aaron: outfield
B. Carlton Fisk: catcher
C. Ryne Sandberg: second base
D. Cal Ripken: shortstop

5.14 **Which NL reliever did not yield a home run in a record 269 consecutive innings from 1979 to 1982?**
A. Greg Minton of the Giants
B. Woody Fryman of the Expos
C. Tug McGraw of the Phillies
D. Kent Tekulve of the Pirates

5.15 **Who swiped a record 50 bases in a row without being caught?**
A. Paul Molitor
B. Tim Raines
C. Vince Coleman
D. Rickey Henderson

5.16 **Who holds the record for fanning the most hitters while pitching a nine-inning no-hitter?**
A. Vida Blue
B. Nolan Ryan
C. Bob Gibson
D. Bert Blyleven

5.17 **Who swatted a record six grand slams in one season?**
A. Jose Canseco
B. Don Mattingly
C. Jack Clark
D. Willie McCovey

5.18 **Which NL player tied a record by breaking up five no-hitters during the 1980s?**
A. Terry Puhl of the Astros
B. Eddie Milner of the Reds
C. Johnny Ray of the Pirates
D. Mookie Wilson of the Mets

Answers

THE RECORD REALM

5.1   D. Roberto Clemente of the Pirates

On August 22, 1970, the Pirates and Dodgers were locked in a
1–1 duel in the 16th inning when Clemente ripped a two-out
single to right for his fifth hit of the day. He then stole second
and scored on a single by Milt May. Reliever Bruce Del Canton
protected the lead in the bottom of the frame, and the Bucs
had a 2–1 victory in a game that took four hours and 21 minutes
to play. The two clubs met again the next afternoon. Clemente,
who had just turned 36, would normally have been given the
day off, but with slugger Willie Stargell out with an injury,
Pittsburgh needed him in the lineup. He responded by rapping five more hits, the last a booming homer in the eighth, as
the Bucs romped to an 11–0 triumph. It marked the first time
in the 20th century that a player had collected five hits in two
straight games.

5.2   B. Wade Boggs

Other players have tallied more 200-hit seasons than Boggs did,
but no one else has managed it seven years in a row, as he did from
1983 to 1989. The Boston bat artist's best season was 1985, when
he stroked 240 safeties, the most in the majors since 1930.

5.3   B. Graig Nettles

Long before he attracted national attention with his hot-corner
heroics in the 1978 World Series, Nettles was an accomplished
glove man. In 1971, with the Cleveland Indians, he established
major-league records for both double plays (54) and assists (412)

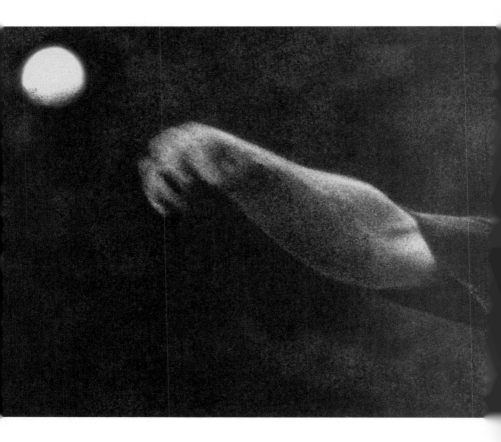

by a third baseman. Although Nettles led all AL third-sackers in assists in 1971, 1972, 1973, 1975 and 1976, he did not win a Gold Glove in any of those years, losing four times to Brooks Robinson and once to Aurelio Rodriguez. However, he did win the award in 1977 and 1978, when the Yankees won the World Series.

5.4   B. Tom Seaver

On April 22, 1970, Seaver took the mound at Shea Stadium and fanned 19 San Diego Padres to match Steve Carlton's record for most strikeouts in a nine-inning game. That mark was later surpassed by Roger Clemens, but another record that Seaver set in the game still stands. The Mets hurler fanned the last ten men

Tom Seaver: He won five NL strikeout crowns in the 1970s.

he faced—the most consecutive strikeouts in history. His effort eclipsed Mickey Welch's 1884 mark of nine in a row. Seaver won the game 2–1, tossing a two-hitter.

5.5   C. He collected seven hits
On September 16, 1975, at Wrigley Field, the Pittsburgh Pirates trounced the Chicago Cubs 22–0. Leading the hit parade was second-baseman Rennie Stennett, who rapped a triple, two doubles and four singles in seven at-bats. The Bucs attack was so relentless that Stennett got two hits in both the first and fifth innings. The only other player to get seven hits in a nine-inning game was Baltimore's Wilbert Robinson in 1895.

5.6   D. Nate Colbert of the Padres

To set this record, it helps to be the only power hitter on a weak team. Colbert and the Padres qualify on both counts. The 1972 Padres are the only postexpansion team to score less than 500 runs in a full season. Without Colbert, they might not have even reached 400. Colbert hit 38 homers; Leron Lee, with 12, was the only other Padre in double digits. Colbert drove in 111 runs; Lee was second with 47. All told, Colbert drove in 22.75 percent of the 488 runs that the Padres pushed across the plate.

DRIVING IN THE HIGHEST PERCENTAGE OF A TEAM'S RUNS*

Player	Year	Team	Team's Runs	Player's RBI	Pct
Nate Colbert	1972	Padres	488	111	22.75
Wally Berger	1935	Braves	575	130	22.61
Ernie Banks	1959	Cubs	673	143	21.25
Jim Gentile	1961	Orioles	691	141	20.41
Bill Nicholson	1943	Cubs	632	128	20.25
Frank Howard	1968	Senators	524	106	20.23
Babe Ruth	1919	Red Sox	564	114	20.21

*CURRENT TO 1998

5.7   B. Hal McRae of the Royals

McRae led the AL with 133 RBI in 1982, while appearing in 158 games as the Royals' DH. No other full-time DH has ever driven in as many runs. It's surprising that McRae would hold this record because 1982 was the only time in his 19-year career in which he drove in 100 runs. Don Baylor had 139 RBI in 1979, but Baylor played more games (97) in the outfield than at DH (65).

5.8   D. Ryne Sandberg

Sandberg is better remembered for his hitting than his glove work, but that's only because he was such an extraordinary offensive threat for a second baseman. In his MVP year in 1984, Sandberg amassed 36 doubles, 19 triples and 19 homers and had a .520

slugging average. In 1990, he swatted 40 homers to join Rogers Hornsby as the only second baseman since the end of the dead ball era to pace his league in four-baggers. On defense, Sandberg was equally spectacular. He won nine Gold Gloves, a record for his position, and his .990 career fielding average tops all second-sackers. In 1989 and 1990, Sandberg set a major-league record for his position by playing 123 consecutive errorless games. During that skein, he also set a record for most chances accepted (582) without a miscue.

5.9 B. Bobby Bonds

The San Francisco outfielder broke his own record of 187 strike-outs by fanning 189 times in 1970. Bonds was the Giants' leadoff hitter, a peculiar position in the batting order for such a free swinger. Despite his alarming strikeout total, he actually had a banner season, batting .302, collecting 200 hits and scoring 134 runs. If you count only the times Bonds made contact with the ball, he hit .422, which suggests he could have had a truly amazing year if he had been more selective at the plate. As it is, Bonds is the only player to hit .300 while recording more than 160 strikeouts.

MOST STRIKEOUTS IN A SEASON*

Player	Year	Team	AB	AVG	SO
Bobby Bonds	1970	Giants	663	.302	189
Bobby Bonds	1969	Giants	622	.259	187
Rob Deer	1987	Brewers	474	.238	186
Pete Incaviglia	1986	Rangers	540	.250	185
Cecil Fielder	1990	Tigers	573	.277	182
Mike Schmidt	1975	Phillies	562	.249	180
Rob Deer	1986	Brewers	466	.232	179

*CURRENT TO 1998

5.10 D. Mike Marshall of the Dodgers

Marshall set a big-league record by appearing in 92 games with the Montreal Expos in 1973. In 1974, with the Dodgers, he pushed the envelope even farther, making 106 trips to the mound and pitching 208 innings. Marshall credited his amazing durability to his own theories on physical conditioning, which he had acquired while earning a Ph.D. in kinesiology, a science concerned with energy and body movement. The reliever's specialty pitch was a screwball, which some would say also described his personality. His maverick ideas often caused conflicts with pitching coaches and managers, but no one could quarrel with his results in 1974. Marshall appeared in 65 percent of the Dodgers games, posted a 15–12 record, 21 saves and a 2.42 ERA and won the Cy Young.

MOST GAMES PITCHED IN A SEASON*

Pitcher	Year	Team	Games	IP	ERA
Mike Marshall	1974	Dodgers	106	208	2.42
Kent Tekulve	1979	Pirates	94	134	2.75
Mike Marshall	1973	Expos	92	179	2.66
Kent Tekulve	1978	Pirates	91	135	2.33
Wayne Granger	1969	Reds	90	144	2.80
Mike Marshall	1979	Twins	90	142	2.65
Kent Tekulve	1987	Phillies	90	105	3.09

*CURRENT TO 1998

5.11 A. He retired 41 batters in a row

Jim Barr may not be a household name, but he holds one of the majors' more impressive records. In a game against the Pirates on August 23, 1972, the 24-year-old Giants rookie retired the last 21 batters he faced. In his next start, a 3–0 win over the Cardinals on August 29, he dispatched the first 20 men to come to the plate, before allowing a double to Bernie Carbo. By setting down 41 straight batters, Barr pitched the equivalent of 13 ⅔ perfect innings.

5.12 D. 35

Stealing bases is not an easy task. Your body takes a severe pounding. Kansas City Royals speedster Willie Wilson once compared the sensation to "jumping out of car that's going 20 miles per hour." Yet, Lou Brock was three months past his 35th birthday when he stole his 105th base of the 1974 season to break Maury Wills's major-league record. Brock went on to pilfer 118 bases, which is still the NL record. No other player over 30 has ever stolen 100 bases. It is hard to understand how Brock did it at age 35.

5.13 A. Hank Aaron: outfield
Babe Ruth owns the mark for most homers by an outfielder, with 686. Ruth hit the other 28 of his 714 homers while serving as a pitcher or at first base. Aaron ranks second, with 661 homers as an outfielder. Aaron hit the rest of his 755 homers while playing another position or in the role of designated hitter.

5.14 A. Greg Minton of the Giants
One of the most valued traits of a reliever is an ability to keep the ball in the park. No fireman has ever been so effective at denying homers as Minton was with the San Francisco Giants from 1979 to 1982. The sinkerballer did not allow a home run in 269 straight innings, the equivalent of almost 30 nine-inning games.

5.15 C. Vince Coleman
Coleman was so explosively fast he could overcome mistakes that would have doomed other base runners. In 1987, for example, he stole second successfully 19 consecutive times *on pitchouts*. During 1988 and 1989, the Cardinals speed merchant raced his way into the record books by swiping 50 bases in 50 attempts, before finally being cut down by Expos catcher Nelson Santovenia.

5.16 B. Nolan Ryan
On July 15, 1973, Ryan tossed his second no-hitter of the season, fanning 17 and walking four, in a 6–0 whitewashing of the Detroit Tigers. Ryan struck out eight straight Tigers at one point and had 16 Ks after seven innings, putting him in range of 19 or 20, but his muscles stiffened up during a 30-minute-long, eighth-inning rally by the Angels, and he struck out only one more batter in the last two frames. Ryan was so overpowering that Norm Cash jokingly took a piano leg up to the plate with two outs in the ninth inning. When the laughter had subsided, umpire Ron Luciano

made Cash return to the dugout to get some legal lumber and he popped out to end the game. In Ryan's next start against the Orioles, he carried a no-hitter into the eighth inning before Mark Belanger spoiled it with a bloop single.

MOST STRIKEOUTS IN A NINE-INNING NO-HITTER*

Pitcher	Date	Team	Opponent	SO
Nolan Ryan	July 15/73	Angels	Tigers	17
Nolan Ryan	May 1/91	Rangers	Blue Jays	16
Nolan Ryan	Sept 28/74	Angels	Twins	15
Don Wilson	June 18/67	Astros	Braves	15
Warren Spahn	Sept 16/60	Braves	Phillies	15

*CURRENT TO 1998

5.17 B. Don Mattingly

In 1987, the number of home runs hit in the majors jumped by 17 percent from the previous year, to a record 4,458. Front and center in the long-ball barrage was Mattingly, who ripped dingers in eight straight games in July, equaling Dale Long's 1956 mark. On September 29, the Yankees' first baseman continued his assault on the record book, swatting his sixth grand slam of the season to snap the record of five, shared by Ernie Banks (1955) and Jim Gentile (1961). Oddly, they were the only grand slams that Mattingly hit in his entire career.

5.18 B. Eddie Milner of the Reds

Although he had only a .253 career batting average, Milner possessed an uncanny knack for spoiling perfection. The Cincinnati outfielder broke up five no-hitters in a span of five years, including two in 1982 and one each in 1983, 1984 and 1986. Milner tied the major-league record, set by Cesar Tovar, who ruined five no-hitters from 1967 and 1975, four with the Minnesota Twins and one as a member of the Texas Rangers.

T R A D I N G   P L A C E S

Very few players, no matter how celebrated, remain with one team for their entire career. Even immortals such as Babe Ruth, Ty Cobb and Rogers Hornsby changed addresses. Your task here is to match the star with the lesser light for whom he was traded.

(Answers are on page 139)

Rick Wise	Jim Fregosi	Ivan Dejesus	Neil Allen
Dave May	Mike Caldwell	Ken Landreaux	Tom Lawless
Dave Tomlin	Charlie Williams		

1. Hank Aaron (Braves to Brewers) for _____

2. Willie Mays (Giants to Mets) for _____

3. Rod Carew (Twins to Angels) for _____

4. Pete Rose (Expos to Reds) for _____

5. Nolan Ryan (Mets to Angels) for _____

6. Steve Carlton (Cards to Phillies) for _____

7. Willie McCovey (Giants to Padres) for _____

8. Keith Hernandez (Cards to Mets) for _____

9. Gaylord Perry (Rangers to Padres) for _____

10. Ryne Sandberg (Phillies to Cubs) for _____

Johnny Bench:
No catcher could
match his bat
power or his
throwing arm.

Chapter Six

EYES ON THE PRIZE

When Ted Williams first saw Johnny Bench in action in 1968, he called the 20-year-old catcher "a Hall of Famer, for sure." Bench fulfilled that prophecy in 1989, when he was inducted into the Hall of Fame on the first ballot. Regarded by many as the greatest catcher of all time, Bench was the main cog in Cincinnati's "Big Red Machine." The 12-time All-Star won two home-run titles and led the NL in RBI three times. Yet, as good as he was at the plate, Bench was even better behind it. He nabbed ten Gold Gloves and revolutionized the position with his one-handed receiving style and cannonlike arm. "I can throw out any man alive," claimed Bench. In his prime, it was no idle boast. In 41 postseason games from 1970 to 1976, he allowed only two stolen bases. As Bench's Cooperstown plaque notes, he "redefined standards by which catchers are measured."

(Answers are on page 79)

6.1 **Who won the MVP Award at two different positions?**
A. Pete Rose
B. Harmon Killebrew
C. Rod Carew
D. Robin Yount

6.2 **"You gotta believe" was the rallying cry of the New York Mets as they staged a late-season surge to capture the 1973 pennant. Who coined the famous phrase?**
A. Mets manager Yogi Berra
B. Mets pitcher Tug McGraw
C. Mets owner Joan Payson
D. Mets broadcaster Lindsay Nelson

6.3 **Who won three MVP Awards—for the regular season, the League Championship Series and the World Series—in one year?**
A. George Brett
B. Pete Rose
C. Mike Schmidt
D. Willie Stargell

6.4 **Which Cy Young Award recipient set a 20th-century record for winning the highest percentage of his team's games in a season?**
A. Randy Jones of the Padres
B. Ferguson Jenkins of the Cubs
C. Steve Carlton of the Phillies
D. Gaylord Perry of the Indians

6.5 **Who was the first AL player to capture a batting title without hitting a single homer?**
A. Rod Carew
B. Wade Boggs
C. Willie Wilson
D. Carney Lansford

6.6 **Who won a batting crown by hitting a controversial inside-the-park homer in his last at-bat of the season?**
A. Pete Rose of the Reds
B. Bill Madlock of the Pirates
C. Alex Johnson of the Angels
D. George Brett of the Royals

6.7 **Who is the only man to win the MVP Award, but never be picked to play in an All-Star Game?**

A. Don Baylor

B. Kirk Gibson

C. Willie McGee

D. George Foster

6.8 **Who was the first AL relief pitcher to win the Cy Young Award?**

A. Ron Perranoski of the Twins

B. Sparky Lyle of the Yankees

C. Rollie Fingers of the Brewers

D. Willie Hernandez of the Tigers

6.9 **Who played the most games without experiencing a taste of postseason action?**

A. Joe Torre

B. Ron Santo

C. Ernie Banks

D. Buddy Bell

6.10 **Bob Lemon was on his second tour of duty when he managed the New York Yankees to their late-season charge to the pennant in 1978. Which team had fired Lemon earlier that season?**

A. The Texas Rangers

B. The Minnesota Twins

C. The California Angels

D. The Chicago White Sox

6.11 **Which pitcher failed to win the Cy Young Award despite leading his league in wins and strikeouts?**

A. Phil Niekro

B. Ferguson Jenkins

C. Mike Norris

D. Mickey Lolich

6.12 **Who appeared in the most World Series games?**
A. Pete Rose
B. Joe Morgan
C. Steve Garvey
D. Reggie Jackson

6.13 **Who hit the most homers in league championship play?**
A. Reggie Jackson
B. George Brett
C. Steve Garvey
D. Johnny Bench

6.14 **"We Are Family" was the theme song of which World Series champion?**
A. The 1979 Pittsburgh Pirates
B. The 1982 St. Louis Cardinals
C. The 1985 Kansas City Royals
D. The 1988 Los Angeles Dodgers

6.15 **Who rapped five hits in his first World Series game?**
A. Amos Otis of the 1980 Royals
B. Paul Molitor of the 1982 Brewers
C. Alan Trammell of the 1984 Tigers
D. Kirby Puckett of the 1987 Twins

6.16 **Who holds the mark for collecting the most combined hits in a LCS and a World Series?**
A. George Brett of the 1985 Royals
B. Lenny Dykstra of the 1986 Mets
C. Marty Barrett of the 1986 Red Sox
D. Willie McGee of the 1987 Cardinals

6.17 **Who is the only pitcher to clinch a division title for his team by hurling a no-hitter?**
A. Jack Morris of the Tigers
B. Ken Holtzman of the Athletics
C. Mike Scott of the Astros
D. Fernando Valenzuela of the Dodgers

Answers

EYES ON THE PRIZE

6.1   D. Robin Yount

Yount became the Milwaukee Brewers' regular shortstop in 1974 at age 18 and soon developed into one of the best players of his generation. In 1982, he won the AL MVP Award by a landslide as he led the Brewers to the pennant. His offensive production was startling for a shortstop. He batted .331, scored 129 runs, had 114 RBI and paced the loop in hits, doubles and slugging average. In 1984, after playing 1,479 games at shortstop, arm and back problems forced Yount to move to the outfield, where he won a second MVP in 1989.

6.2   B. Mets pitcher Tug McGraw

In mid-August 1973, the Mets were in last place in the NL East, 13 games below .500, when Donald Grant, the team's chairman of the board, made a rare visit to the clubhouse to deliver a pep talk. Grant told the players that it wasn't too late to make a comeback and if they believed in themselves, they could do it. As Grant left the room, relief pitcher Tug McGraw jumped up on a stool and began mimicking the chairman, saying, "You gotta believe, you guys. You gotta believe." But when the Mets suddenly started winning, McGraw's sarcastic outburst was adopted as an inspirational slogan. It even took on holy overtones when nuns began holding up "You Gotta Believe" signs at Shea Stadium. In September, the Mets rallied to overtake the other five teams in the division, finishing one game ahead of the Cardinals, two up on the Pirates and three clear of the Expos. They then upset the powerhouse Cincinnati Reds in the NLCS, before falling to the Oakland A's in the World Series.

79

6.3 **D. Willie Stargell**

Stargell played 18 years before winning his first MVP Award in 1979. Statistically speaking, it was not the most impressive season of his career, but the 39-year-old veteran was the inspirational leader of the pennant-winning Pittsburgh Pirates, and that was the main reason he tied Keith Hernandez in the MVP voting. Stargell's two post-season MVP selections were no-brainers. He batted .455 with two homers and six RBI in the Bucs' three-game sweep of the Reds in the NLCS, and he hit .400 with three homers and seven RBI against Baltimore in the 1979 Fall Classic, including a game-winning two-run shot in the sixth inning of game seven.

6.4 **C. Steve Carlton of the Phillies**

Carlton won four Cy Young Awards, but the most stunning was his first in 1972. Despite toiling for the cellar-dwelling Philadelphia Phillies, the big lefty won a league-high 27 games to equal the NL record for southpaws set by Sandy Koufax in 1966. He also topped the NL with 30 complete games, 310 strikeouts and a 1.97 ERA. Not only was Carlton the first pitcher from a last-place team to lead his league in wins; his 27 victories represented 45.8 percent of the Phillies' team total, a 20th-century record.

HIGHEST PERCENTAGE OF A TEAM'S VICTORIES*

Pitcher	Year	Team	Team Wins	Pitcher Wins	Pct
Steve Carlton	1972	Phillies	59	27	45.8
Ed Walsh	1908	White Sox	88	40	45.5
Jack Chesbro	1904	Yankees	92	41	44.6
Noodles Hahn	1901	Reds	52	22	42.3
Cy Young	1901	Red Sox	79	33	41.8
Cy Young	1902	Red Sox	77	32	41.6
Ed Rommell	1922	Athletics	65	27	41.5
Red Faber	1921	White Sox	62	25	40.3

*1900 TO 1998

6.5 A. Rod Carew

Only three players have won batting titles without hitting a single homer: Ginger Beaumont of the Pirates in 1902, Zack Wheat of the Dodgers in 1918 and Rod Carew of the Twins in 1972. There was nothing unusual about Carew winning batting titles—he captured seven—but 1972 was the only season of his 19-year career that the Panamanian failed to hit at least one homer.

6.6 D. George Brett of the Royals

Brett and teammate Hal McRae's battle for the 1976 AL batting title came down to their last at-bats of the season. Entering the ninth inning of the Royals' last game against the Minnesota Twins, McRae led Brett .3326996 to .3322981. Brett opened the inning by hitting a routine fly to left, but outfielder Steve Brye failed to catch the ball and it bounded over his head for an inside-the-park homer. The tainted hit raised Brett's average to .333. McRae then followed by grounding out to short, to finish the year at .332. McRae, who is black, accused Brye of letting the ball drop so that a white man could win the title. Brye initially denied the charge, saying he had misjudged the ball, but later lent credence to McRae's suspicions by claiming that Brett, a full-time third baseman, was more deserving of the batting title than McRae, who was a designated hitter.

6.7 B. Kirk Gibson

Although the hard-charging outfielder had several fine seasons with the Detroit Tigers in the mid-1980s and won the NL MVP Award in 1988 for his inspirational play with the Los Angeles Dodgers, Gibson was never selected to an All-Star team during his 17-year career. No other MVP winner can make that claim.

6.8 B. Sparky Lyle of the Yankees

"Why pitch nine innings when you can get just as famous pitching two?" asked Lyle. He had a point. Relief pitchers rose to prominence in the 1970s, and the Yankee bullpen ace was at the forefront, becoming the first AL reliever to snag the Cy Young Award in 1977. Appearing in a loop-leading 72 games, the tobacco-chewing lefty went 13–5 with 26 saves and a 2.17 ERA. Lyle's clutch pitching was a major factor in the Yankees winning the pennant, but he also benefited in the balloting for the Cy Young because there was no dominant starter in the AL that year.

6.9 C. Ernie Banks

The best player never to appear in the postseason, the 11-time All-Star played 2,528 games for the Chicago Cubs in his 19-year career. Although it must have been frustrating to spend so many seasons with a loser, you couldn't tell by Banks's demeanor. The ever-smiling and enthusiastic "Mr. Cub" was fond of saying, "It's a great day for baseball. Let's play two today!" His best shot at making the postseason was in 1969, when the Cubs held first place for 155 days, only to be overtaken by the Miracle Mets.

MOST GAMES WITHOUT A POSTSEASON APPEARANCE*

Player	Years	Games
Ernie Banks	1953–71	2,528
Luke Appling	1930–50	2,422
Mickey Vernon	1939–60	2,409
Buddy Bell	1972–89	2,405
Ron Santo	1960–74	2,243
Joe Torre	1960–77	2,209
Toby Harrah	1969–86	2,155

*1903 TO 1998

6.10 D. The Chicago White Sox

After Chicago got off to a slow start in 1978, Lemon was fired by owner Bill Veeck on June 30. Ironically, before dismissing Lemon, Veeck tried unsuccessfully to trade his manager to the Yankees in exchange for Billy Martin. Lemon was hired as the Yankees' skipper on July 25, when Martin was axed by Steinbrenner. His laid-back style proved the perfect tonic for the Yanks, who staged a remarkable comeback, winning 48 of their last 68 games and defeating the Boston Red Sox in a one-game playoff to take the pennant. The pinstripers then went on to win the LCS and the World Series.

6.11   D. Mickey Lolich

Topping the league in wins and strikeouts is normally a sure-fire guarantee of winning the Cy Young Award—unless your name happens to be Mickey Lolich. In 1971, the Detroit Tigers south-paw led the AL in both categories, going 25–14 with 308 strikeouts and a 2.92 ERA, yet he still lost in the balloting to Oakland's Vida Blue, who was 24–8 with 301 strikeouts and a 1.82 ERA.

6.12   A. Pete Rose

Winning teams just seemed to follow Rose around. He appeared in 34 World Series games in six trips to the big show with the Reds and the Phillies. Although that total is miles behind Yogi Berra's record of 75 World Series games, it was the highest of any player during the era. With a little luck, Reggie Jackson, who played in 27 Series contests, could have exceeded Rose's total. In 1972, a pulled hamstring kept Jackson out of the A's seven-game tilt with the Reds, and he saw action in only three of the six games of the 1981 Series for the Yankees because manager Bob Lemon benched him against the Dodgers' lefty starters.

6.13   B. George Brett

Pitcher Rudy May contended that the only way to pitch Brett was "inside, so you force him to pull the ball. That way the line drive won't hit you." Brett's always-dangerous bat was especially destructive in the playoffs. In six league-championship series, the Kansas City Royals star hit .340, ripped nine homers and posted a .728 slugging average. As of 1998, Brett's nine homers are still a record for LCS play.

6.14   A. The 1979 Pittsburgh Pirates

Early in the 1979 season, someone played "We Are Family," the rhythm-and-blues hit recording by the group Sister Sledge, in the Bucs clubhouse. It soon became the team's theme song. The Pirates were a close-knit group of colorful individuals. The lineup included Dave "Cobra" Parker, Bill "Mad Dog" Madlock, Tim "Crazy Horse" Foli, Phil "Scrap Iron" Garner and John "Candy Man" Candelaria. But the guiding influence was the man they called "Pops," 39-year-old MVP winner Willie Stargell. The Pirates demonstrated their resilience and team spirit by rallying from a 3–1 deficit in games in the 1979 Series to defeat the Orioles.

6.15 B. Paul Molitor of the 1982 Brewers

Molitor lived up to his nickname "the Ignitor" in the first game of the 1982 Series. Batting leadoff, he cracked five singles, setting a single-game Series record for hits, as the Brewers crushed the Cardinals 11–0. Molitor collected a total of 11 hits in the Fall Classic, one less than teammate Robin Yount. Yet, despite this formidable one-two punch at the top of its order, Milwaukee lost to St. Louis in seven games.

6.16 C. Marty Barrett of the 1986 Red Sox

Known as a steady but unspectacular second baseman, Barrett stole the postseason spotlight in 1986 with his sizzling bat. He rapped 11 hits in the seven-game LCS with the Angels, then followed that performance up by cracking 13 safeties in a losing cause against the Mets in the World Series. Barrett's 24 hits obliterated George Brett's postseason mark of 18, set in 1985.

6.17 C. Mike Scott of the Astros

On September 25, 1986, the Astros ace upped his record to 18–10 by pitching a 2–0 no-hitter against the San Francisco Giants at the Astrodome. Scott's masterpiece eliminated the Cincinnati Reds— the Astros' last mathematical threat—from contention for the NL West title. The only other pitcher to hurl a no-hitter on the day his team clinched a league title is Allie Reynolds of the Yankees, who stifled the Red Sox on September 28, 1951. But Reynolds's gem didn't sew up the AL pennant outright; it only assured New York of at least a tie for first.

COUNTERFEIT CREDENTIALS

In each of the quartets below, one player does not belong. See if you can find the fake. *(Answers are on page 139)*

1. Hit 300 homers and stole 300 bases:
    Willie Mays, Andre Dawson, Don Baylor, Bobby Bonds

2. Struck out 300 batters in a season:
    Tom Seaver, Steve Carlton, Mike Scott, Mickey Lolich

3. Won an NL MVP Award:
    Joe Torre, Tony Perez, Steve Garvey, Ryne Sandberg

4. Won an AL MVP Award:
    Thurman Munson, Jeff Burroughs, Don Baylor, Alan Trammell

5. Hit 40 homers in a season:
    Tony Armas, Eddie Murray, Davey Johnson, Dale Murphy

6. Collected 3,000 career hits:
    Al Kaline, Lou Brock, George Brett, Frank Robinson

7. Recorded 3,000 career strikeouts:
    Bob Gibson, Ferguson Jenkins, Mickey Lolich, Bert Blyleven

8. Won an NL batting crown:
    Joe Torre, Jose Cruz, Tim Raines, Keith Hernandez

9. Led the AL in ERA:
    Luis Tiant, Dave Stieb, Catfish Hunter, Nolan Ryan

10. Was elected to the Hall of Fame on the first ballot:
    Juan Marichal, Ernie Banks, Willie Stargell, Joe Morgan

Vida Blue:
He was the
youngest player
to capture an
MVP award.

Chapter Seven

TRUE OR FALSE?

Vida Blue was the only American League pitcher to win an All-Star Game from 1963 to 1982. True or False? Incredibly, it's true. The AL's lone victory in the 19-year span was in 1971. Blue, the starter in that year's game, was a fitting candidate for the honor. Armed with a flaming fastball, the 21-year-old southpaw had blazed through the first half of the season like a streaking comet. After losing his first start, Blue won ten straight, all complete games in which he allowed six hits or less; five of them shutouts. By the All-Star break, he had 17 wins against only three defeats and was baseball's biggest attraction. Even though his pace slowed in the second half, Blue's final stats were awesome: a 24–8 record, 301 strike-outs and a 1.82 ERA. By year's end, he owned two new trophies: the MVP and the Cy Young. *(Answers are on page 90)*

7.1   Nolan Ryan never won a Cy Young Award. **True or False?**

7.2   No player has ever hit fewer than 150 homers and struck out more than 1,500 times. **True or False?**

7.3 Willie Mays played in more All-Star Games than he played seasons. **True or False?**

7.4 Tom Seaver never pitched a no-hitter. **True or False?**

7.5 Reggie Jackson has the lowest career batting average of any outfielder elected to the Hall of Fame. **True or False?**

7.6 Despite his reputation for throwing spitballs, Gaylord Perry was never ejected from a game for doctoring a baseball. **True or False?**

7.7 Mike Schmidt led the NL in homers more often than any other player in history. **True or False?**

7.8 Pete Rose posted more 200-hit seasons than any other player in history. **True or False?**

7.9 Nolan Ryan broke Sandy Koufax's single-season strikeout record with his last pitch of the 1973 season. **True or False?**

7.10 Don Mattingly holds the New York Yankees record for most hits in a season. **True or False?**

7.11 Frank Robinson was the first black manager in both the AL and the NL. **True or False?**

7.12 Dick Williams managed the Oakland Athletics to three straight World Series titles. **True or False?**

7.13 The covers of all the baseballs used in the major leagues must be made of horsehide. **True or False?**

7.14 Willie Mays made more career putouts than any other outfielder. **True or False?**

7.15 No designated hitter has ever won the Rookie of the Year Award. **True or False?**

7.16   Brooks Robinson of the Baltimore Orioles holds the record for playing the most games with one team. **True or False?**

7.17   No player has ever hit a ball out of the Minnesota Metrodome. **True or False?**

7.18   None of the original members of the 1962 New York Mets were with the club when it won the 1969 World Series. **True or False?**

7.19   Joe Niekro hit his only homer off his brother Phil. **True or False?**

7.20   Andre Dawson is the only player to win the MVP Award with a last-place team. **True or False?**

7.21   The pitcher who holds the record for winning the most games by the All-Star break was not named to the midseason All-Star squad that year. **True or False?**

7.22   Nolan Ryan does *not* hold the record for most career strikeouts in either the AL or NL. **True or False?**

7.23   Rollie Fingers holds the record for most games pitched in World Series play. **True or False?**

7.24   Mickey Mantle and Willie Mays were both banned from baseball after they retired as players. **True or False?**

7.25   Nolan Ryan never pitched in a World Series. **True or False?**

7.26   Bucky Dent hit the homer that provided the New York Yankees with the winning run in their 1978 playoff game against the Boston Red Sox. **True or False?**

7.27   Steve Carlton was the first pitcher to break Walter Johnson's career record for strikeouts. **True or False?**

7.28   Pete Rose holds the record for the most plate appearances in a season without stealing a single base. **True or False?**

Answers

T R U E   O R   F A L S E ?

7.1 **True**

Nolan Ryan never won baseball's most prestigious pitching honor. He came closest in 1973, when he fanned 383 batters to break Sandy Koufax's single-season strikeout mark and posted a 21–16 won–lost record and a 2.87 ERA. That year, Ryan finished second in the voting to Jim Palmer of the Baltimore Orioles, who was 22–9 with 2.40 ERA and 158 strikeouts.

7.2 **False**

Lou Brock hit only 149 homers, yet he struck out 1,730 times, eighth on the all-time whiff list, just ahead of Mickey Mantle and Harmon Killebrew. None of the other 18 players with 1,500 strikeouts hit fewer than 200 round-trippers. In fact, only one player on the list—Rick Monday—hit less than 300.

7.3 **True**

Willie Mays made his 24th and final All-Star appearance as a pinch-hitter in 1973, striking out against Sparky Lyle. Mays was able to play in more All-Star Games than he played seasons, because from 1957 to 1962 there were two games staged each summer.

7.4 **False**

For a long time Tom Seaver seemed jinxed in his quest to pitch a no-hitter. He came close several times, tossing four one-hitters with the Mets, including two heartbreakers against the Chicago Cubs. On July 9, 1969, Seaver lost both a no-hitter and a perfect

90

game when Jim Qualls rapped a pinch-double with one out in the ninth inning. On September 24, 1975, pinch-hitter Joe Wallis singled with two outs in the ninth to foil another no-hit bid. Seaver finally recorded the only no-hitter of his career with the Cincinnati Reds on June 16, 1978, when he blanked the Cardinals 4–0 at Riverfront Stadium.

7.5   True

Reggie Jackson's career .262 batting average is easily the worst of any outfielder in the Hall of Fame. The closest contender is Ralph Kiner, who batted .279. In fact, Jackson is tied with Luis Aparicio for the fourth-lowest average of any Hall of Famer.

LOWEST BATTING AVERAGES BY HALL OF FAMERS*

Player	Years	Pos	Avg
Ray Schalk	1912–29	C	.253
Harmon Killebrew	1954–75	1B/3B	.256
Rabbit Maranville	1912–35	SS	.258
Luis Aparicio	1956–73	SS	.262
Reggie Jackson	1967–87	OF	.262
Joe Tinker	1902–16	SS	.263

*CURRENT TO 1998

7.6   False

Gaylord Perry had the audacity to publish his autobiography, *Me and the Spitter*, in 1973, while he was still an active player. In the book, Perry discussed his quest for the ideal lubricant for throwing spitballs. But even before this revelation, everyone suspected that Perry threw the wet one and umpires were constantly trying to catch him in the act. He was routinely frisked on the mound, toweled off and forced to change clothes in mid-game. When Billy Martin was managing the Detroit Tigers, he once brought a bloodhound trained to sniff Vaseline to the park when Perry was scheduled to pitch. Even so, it was not until August 23, 1982, while pitching for the Seattle Mariners, that Perry was finally ejected from a game for throwing a spitter. By that point he had been in the majors for 21 years and had more than 300 wins. The penalty? A ten-day suspension and a $250 fine. Not too steep a price to pay for a brilliant career.

7.7 True

A three-time MVP winner, Mike Schmidt was the premier third baseman and leading slugger in the National League for much of the 1970s and 1980s. The Phillies' superstar racked up 13 seasons of 30 homers or more, while amassing 548 career dingers. Schmidt led the NL in four-baggers a record eight times. Only Babe Ruth won more homer crowns.

MOST HOME-RUN TITLES*

Player	Years	League	Titles	Led Majors
Babe Ruth	22	AL	12	11
Mike Schmidt	18	NL	8	6
Ralph Kiner	10	NL	7	6
Harmon Killebrew	22	AL	6	4
Gavvy Cravath	11	NL	6	4
Mel Ott	22	NL	6	0

*CURRENT TO 1998

7.8 True

Pete Rose reached the 200-hit mark ten times during his career, the last coming in 1979, when he banged out 208 hits for the Phillies to snap Ty Cobb's record of nine.

7.9 True

When Nolan Ryan took the mound for his last start of the 1973 season, he needed 15 strikeouts to equal Sandy Koufax's single-season record of 382 strikeouts. The Angels' opponents, the Minnesota Twins, nearly knocked Ryan out of the box in the early going, but after a shaky couple of innings "the Express" got rolling. When he fanned Steve Brye in the eighth inning, it gave

Pete Rose: His game was ferocity and flat-out hustle.

him 15 Ks and a share of the record. However, Ryan, who was
suffering from leg cramps, did not get a strikeout in the ninth.
Fortunately for him, the game was tied 4-4 and went into extra
innings. Ryan again failed to post a strikeout in the tenth, but the
game remained tied. With two outs in the 11th, Rod Carew drew a
walk and Minnesota sent up pinch-hitter Rich Reese. Ryan fanned
Reese on three pitches to surpass Koufax. Because the Angels
scored in the bottom of the 11th to win the game 5-4, Ryan set the
record with his last pitch of 1973. It's worth noting that Ryan set
his record in the first year of the DH. If pitchers had been batting
that season, his total could have easily been up around 425.

7.10   True

Don Mattingly set two Yankees hitting records in 1986. The classy pinstriper drilled 238 hits, to break Earle Combs's single-season mark of 231, and he also cracked 53 doubles, to break Lou Gehrig's franchise standard of 49.

7.11   True

Frank Robinson made managerial history twice: in 1974, when he signed with the Cleveland Indians to become the majors' first black manager; and in 1981, when he took the helm of the San Francisco Giants to become the first black manager in NL annals.

7.12   False

The Oakland Athletics won three straight World Series titles from 1972 to 1974, but Dick Williams managed the club for only the first two. Alvin Dark piloted the A's in 1974. Exasperated by the antics of owner Charlie Finley, Williams left Oakland in December 1973 and signed to manage the New York Yankees. But Williams still had one year left on his Oakland contract, and Finley sued the Yankees. After fierce legal wrangling, the league ruled in Finley's favor and Williams sat out the first half of 1974, before returning to assume the helm of the California Angels.

7.13   False

Prior to 1975, all baseballs used in the majors were made of horsehide, but that year a shortage in the supply of horsehide from Eastern Europe caused a change in the rules; for the first time, ball covers could be composed of cowhide. Since 1977, when Rawlings Sporting Goods became the majors' sole supplier of baseballs, all balls have been made from cowhide.

7.14   True

Willie Mays wielded a titanic bat, but it was his dazzling fielding and base running that earned him the reputation as baseball's most exciting player. Patrolling center field with grace and flair, he tracked down every fly ball that was humanly possible to catch, plus a few that weren't. Mays retired with 7,095 putouts, the most by an outfielder.

7.15 False

Conventional strategy dictates that you make power-hitting, poor-fielding veterans your designated hitters, but Baltimore Orioles manager Earl Weaver broke with traditional thinking in 1977. Rather than replace veteran Lee May at first base, he had rookie first-sacker Eddie Murray serve as the Orioles' DH for the bulk of the season. Murray's impressive batting stats (283 average, 27 homers, 88 RBI), enabled him to edge Oakland outfielder Mitchell Page for AL Rookie of the Year. The following season, Murray inherited the first-base job from May, who moved to DH.

7.16 False

The record for most games played for one team belongs to Carl Yastrzemski, who appeared in 3,308 games for the Boston Red Sox from 1961 to 1983. Brooks Robinson ranks fourth, although he shares the mark for most seasons with one team (23) with Yaz.

MOST GAMES WITH ONE TEAM*

Player	Team	Years	Games
Carl Yastrzemski	Red Sox	23	3,308
Hank Aaron	Braves	21	3,076
Stan Musial	Cardinals	22	3,026
Brooks Robinson	Orioles	23	2,896
Willie Mays	Giants	20	2,857
Robin Yount	Brewers	20	2,856
Al Kaline	Tigers	22	2,834

*CURRENT TO 1998

7.17 False

Dave "Kong" Kingman was known as a power hitter, but no one could have envisioned him hitting a ball out of a domed stadium. Yet that's exactly what the six-foot-six, 210-pound Oakland A's slugger did on May 4, 1984, at Minnesota's Metrodome. Kingman hit a towering pop fly that went through an eight-inch-wide tear in the canvas roof. The ball never returned to the playing field, and

Kingman was credited with a ground-rule double. The next day, a maintenance worker crawled up on the roof and dislodged the ball. It now resides in the Baseball Hall of Fame.

7.18 False

Gil Hodges, the New York Mets manager in 1969, played 54 games for the Mets in the team's first season in 1962, and 11 more games in 1963, before retiring to become the skipper of the Washington Senators. Hodges returned to New York to manage the Mets in 1968. Pitcher Al Jackson, another member of the original Mets, was with the club at the start of the 1969 season, but he was traded to Cincinnati in June.

7.19 True

What are the odds? On May 29, 1976, Houston Astros hurler Joe Niekro hit his first and only big-league homer off his brother Phil, who was pitching for the Atlanta Braves. The blow tied the game, and Houston went on to a 4–3 victory. Joe got the win and Phil took the loss.

7.20 True

Logically, a player with a cellar-dweller shouldn't win the MVP Award. But Andre Dawson's 49 homers and 137 RBI for the Chicago Cubs in 1987 were imposing enough to make the voters set aside logic. Although Chicago did finish last in the NL East, it was not the NL's worst team: the club's 76 wins would have placed them third in the NL West. Fittingly, the only other player to win the MVP Award with a losing team was also a Cub. Ernie Banks snagged the trophy in 1958 and 1959, despite playing for Chicago squads with sub-.500 records.

7.21 True

Wilbur Wood of the Chicago White Sox had 18 wins when the 1973 All-Star Game was played on July 24, yet he was not picked for the AL All-Star team. No other hurler has had so many victories by the All-Star break. The fact that Wood also had 14 losses undoubtedly contributed to his exclusion from the roster, but it's still an amazing snub. Wood went on to log a 24–20 mark in 1973.

7.22 **True**

Despite being the majors' all-time strikeout leader, Nolan Ryan does not hold the strikeout mark for either league. His career was too evenly split between the two circuits: 14 seasons in the NL and 12 seasons in the AL. As of 1998, Ryan stood second on the AL strikeout chart, behind Walter Johnson, and tenth on the NL list, behind leader Steve Carlton.

CAREER STRIKEOUT LEADERS*

American League Pitcher	SO	National League Pitcher	SO
Walter Johnson	3,508	Steve Carlton	4,000
Nolan Ryan	3,355	Tom Seaver	3,272
Roger Clemens	3,153	Bob Gibson	3,117
Bert Blyleven	3,079	Don Sutton	2,939
Mickey Lolich	2,679	Phil Niekro	2,912
Frank Tanana	2,669	Warren Spahn	2,583
Bob Feller	2,581	Christy Mathewson	2,502

*CURRENT TO 1998

7.23 **False**

The Oakland A's played 19 games in three trips to the World Series during the 1970s, and reliever Rollie Fingers pitched in 16 of them, but that still left him six games shy of Whitey Ford's record. The Yankee great *started* 22 games in Series competition.

7.24 **True**

When Willie Mays accepted a public-relations job with an Atlantic City casino in 1979, baseball commissioner Bowie Kuhn banned Mays from baseball. Claiming he was worried about Mays consorting with gamblers, Kuhn said that "such associations by people in our game are inconsistent with its best interest." A few years later, when Mickey Mantle was hired as director of sports programs by another Atlantic City casino, Kuhn forced Mantle out of baseball. In 1985, Peter Ueberroth, Kuhn's successor, removed the ban and welcomed Mays and Mantle back into the fold. "The world changes," said Ueberroth. "I don't think we can start dictating who you can play golf with."

7.25   False

Nolan Ryan made one relief appearance in game three of the 1969 World Series for the New York Mets. He pitched 2 ⅓ scoreless innings to combine with starter Gary Gentry on a 5–0 shutout.

7.26   False

Bucky Dent's dramatic, three-run homer in the seventh inning put the Yankees ahead 4–2 in their 1978 playoff tilt with the Red Sox. However, it was Reggie Jackson's solo shot in the eighth inning that supplied the winning run. The Red Sox rallied to score twice in the bottom of the eighth to make the score 5–4. If not for Jackson's blow, Boston might have gone on to win the game.

7.27   False

Nolan Ryan was the first to break Walter Johnson's career strikeout mark. The record fell on April 27, 1983, when the Astros righty made Brad Mills of the Expos his 3,509th strikeout victim. Steve Carlton passed Johnson's mark three weeks later, on May 20. By the end of the 1983 season, Carlton actually had more career strikeouts than Ryan, but after that point Ryan pulled away.

7.28   True

Few teams go far without a leadoff hitter who steals bases. The 1975 Cincinnati Reds were an exception to the rule. Cincy won the World Series even though its leadoff man, Peter Rose, failed to swipe a single bag. Rose attempted only one steal during the season, despite an astounding 764 plate appearances—the most ever by a player with zero steals. He certainly had ample opportunity to run. Rose collected 210 hits and 89 walks and was hit by a pitch 11 times, to reach base 310 times. Even if we deduct his homers and triples from the total, he still had 299 chances to steal. You have to wonder what happened to his famous hustle.

C L O S I N G   T H E   D E A L

By the 1970s, every successful team had a relief specialist who could be counted on to snuff out opposition rallies and preserve wins. Match the bullpen aces listed below with their stats from the season in which they posted their career high for saves.   *(Answers are on page 139)*

Bruce Sutter   John Hiller   Kent Tekulve
Goose Gossage   Jeff Reardon   Dave Righetti
Rollie Fingers   Sparky Lyle   Dan Quisenberry

	G	IP	W	L	SO	BB	ERA	SAV
1. _____	74	106	8	8	83	35	2.45	46
2. _____	69	139	5	3	48	11	1.94	45
3. _____	71	122	5	7	77	23	1.54	45
4. _____	63	73	2	4	56	15	2.47	42
5. _____	65	125	10	5	124	39	1.44	38
6. _____	67	107	6	13	72	29	2.52	37
7. _____	59	108	9	5	75	29	1.91	35
8. _____	64	99	6	2	103	37	2.27	33
9. _____	91	135	8	7	77	55	2.33	31

Dwight Gooden:
At age 19,
he fanned a
rookie record
276 batters.

Chapter Eight

YOUNG LIONS

No rookie has ever made a more explosive impact than Dwight Gooden. Armed with a high-riding fastball and a snapping curve, the New York Mets phenom posted a 17–9 record, a 2.60 ERA and 276 strikeouts in only 218 innings—the most strikeouts in the majors in 1984, and a record for rookies. Even more amazing was the 19-year-old's average of 11.4 strikeouts per nine innings. Not even such fabled flamethrowers as Bob Feller, Sandy Koufax or Nolan Ryan had ever averaged 11 punch-outs per game for a season. In 1987, Ryan would edge past Gooden's mark, recording 270 strikeouts in 211 innings, a rate of 11.5 whiffs per game. But for one glittering season, a bone-lean black kid from Florida was baseball's king of Ks.

In this chapter, we showcase the era's young lions: some who fulfilled their great expectations, and some who did not.

(Answers are on page 105)

8.1 **Who fanned a record 15 batters in his first game in the majors?**
A. J.R. Richard
B. Don Gullett
C. Jack Morris
D. Frank Tanana

8.2 **Who was the first rookie to capture an MVP Award?**
A. Fred Lynn
B. Dwight Gooden
C. Cal Ripken
D. No rookie has ever won the award

8.3 **Who holds the rookie record for hitting safely in the most consecutive games?**
A. Wade Boggs
B. Will Clark
C. Ryne Sandberg
D. Benito Santiago

8.4 **How many home runs did Mark McGwire hit in his first season?**
A. 19
B. 29
C. 39
D. 49

8.5 **Which player broke into the majors after serving six years in prison for armed robbery?**
A. Ralph Garr of the Braves
B. Enos Cabell of the Astros
C. Ron LeFlore of the Tigers
D. George Hendrick of the Indians

8.6 **Who was the only rookie from the era to post a 20-win season?**
A. Mark Fidrych of the Tigers
B. Mike Boddicker of the Orioles
C. Tom Browning of the Reds
D. Rick Sutcliffe of the Dodgers

8.7 **Which speedster holds the single-season record for stolen bases by a freshman?**
A. Omar Moreno
B. Tim Raines
C. Bill North
D. Vince Coleman

8.8 **Who hit 19 triples in his rookie season—the most three-baggers by a first-year player since Paul Waner hit 22 in 1926?**
A. Juan Samuel of the Phillies
B. Gary Templeton of the Cardinals
C. Amos Otis of the Royals
D. Mickey Rivers of the Angels

8.9 **Who is the youngest pitcher to win the Cy Young Award?**
A. Vida Blue
B. Bret Saberhagen
C. Dwight Gooden
D. Fernando Valenzuela

8.10 **Who did not allow an earned run in the first 34 innings he pitched in the majors?**
A. Frank Tanana of the Angels
B. Dennis Eckersley of the Indians
C. Fernando Valenzuela of the Dodgers
D. John Candelaria of the Pirates

8.11 **Which outfielder was also selected in the NBA, ABA and NFL drafts?**
A. Al Cowens
B. Larry Herndon
C. Dave Winfield
D. George Foster

8.12 **Which Rookie of the Year was nicknamed after a character on the children's TV show *Sesame Street*?**
A. Dwight Gooden
B. Mark Fidrych
C. Carlton Fisk
D. Andre Dawson

8.13 **Which future superstar hit a lowly .196 in his first season?**
A. Mike Schmidt
B. Tony Gwynn
C. Kirby Puckett
D. Don Mattingly

8.14 Who finished third in the voting for Rookie of the Year, despite batting .349?
A. Bill Madlock
B. Juan Samuel
C. Wade Boggs
D. Paul Molitor

8.15 Which Rookie of the Year was also named *The Sporting News'* College Player of the Year earlier in the same season?
A. Bob Horner
B. Steve Sax
C. Dave Righetti
D. Lou Whitaker

8.16 Which rookie came within five innings of becoming the only AL relief pitcher to win an ERA crown?
A. Ron Davis of the Yankees
B. Terry Forster of the White Sox
C. Steve Foucault of the Rangers
D. Mark Eichorn of the Blue Jays

8.17 Who holds the big-league record for most saves by a first-year pitcher?
A. Gregg Olson of the Orioles
B. Dan Quisenberry of the Royals
C. Steve Howe of the Dodgers
D. Todd Worrell of the Cardinals

8.18 Which player had been the property of five teams by the time he won the award for Rookie of the Year?
A. Chris Chambliss
B. Bake McBride
C. Lou Piniella
D. Mike Hargrove

Answers

YOUNG LIONS

8.1   **A. J.R. Richard**

On September 5, 1971, the Houston Astros sent a six-foot-eight-inch rookie from Vienna, Louisiana, named James Rodney Richard to the mound to face the San Francisco Giants. Displaying a terrifying fastball and a wicked slider, Richard fanned 15 Giants in his big-league debut to tie the record for Ks by a pitcher in his first start, set by the Dodgers' Karl Spooner in 1954. Among Richard's victims was Willie Mays, who after whiffing for the third time took himself out of the game, saying, "Nobody ever struck out Willie Mays four times in a game. I ain't playing anymore."

8.2   **A. Fred Lynn**

Lynn enjoyed a spectacular freshman season in 1975. The Red Sox center fielder hit .331, led the AL in runs (103), doubles (47) and slugging average (.566). He also thumped 21 homers and 105 RBI and copped a Gold Glove. Lynn won the MVP and Rookie of the Year Awards by a landslide—the only player to nab both awards in the same season. Unfortunately, Lynn failed to fulfill his incredible promise. Injuries prevented him from ever playing a full season, and with the exception of one more stellar year in 1979, the rest of his career, while respectable, was considered a disappointment in the light of his brilliant beginning.

8.3   **D. Benito Santiago**

By rapping hits in 34 consecutive games in 1987, the San Diego Padres catcher erased a rookie record that had remained undisturbed since 1899, when Pittsburgh Pirates rookie third baseman

Jimmy Williams notched hits in 29 straight games. Santiago's hitting streak was not just the longest by a rookie, it was also the longest streak by a catcher in major-league history.

8.4 D. 49

Mark McGwire gave early notice of his prodigious power, dialing long distance 49 times as a rookie with Oakland in 1987. His effort demolished Al Rosen's AL record of 37 homers and the major-league mark of 38, shared by Frank Robinson and Wally Berger. McGwire might have hit 50, if he had not opted to miss the last game of the season to be present at the birth of his son.

MOST HOME RUNS BY ROOKIES*

Player	Year	Team	AB	AVG	HR
Mark McGwire	1987	Athletics	557	.289	49
Frank Robinson	1956	Reds	572	.290	38
Wally Berger	1930	Braves	555	.310	38
Al Rosen	1950	Indians	554	.287	37
Mike Piazza	1993	Dodgers	547	.318	35
Rudy York	1937	Tigers	375	.307	35
Hal Trosky	1934	Indians	625	.330	35
Ron Kittle	1983	White Sox	520	.254	35

*CURRENT TO 1998

8.5 C. Ron LeFlore of the Tigers

LeFlore, who grew up in the crime-infested projects of East Detroit, was a superb natural athlete. But he didn't develop his talents until he began playing for the baseball team at Southern Michigan State Prison, where he was serving a five-to-15 stretch for armed robbery. Prison friends wrote to the Detroit Tigers raving about LeFlore's skills, and Tigers manager Billy Martin eventually visited the prison, met LeFlore and invited him to try out with the team after he was paroled. When he did, LeFlore so impressed the Tigers with his speed, power and throwing arm that they signed him to a contract. After a brief stint in the minors, he was called up in 1974 and became the club's center fielder. In 1976, LeFlore started in left field at the All-Star Game.

8.6 C. Tom Browning of the Reds

In 1985, Browning became the first rookie to win 20 games since the Yankees' Bob Grim in 1954. The 25-year-old native of Casper, Wyoming, was the linchpin of Cincinnati's pitching staff, starting 38 games and logging a 20–9 record in 261 innings. Even so, Browning placed second in the balloting for NL Rookie of the Year, behind the Cardinals' Vince Coleman.

8.7 D. Vince Coleman

The fleet-footed Cardinals leadoff hitter gave pitchers fits in his debut season in 1985, swiping 110 bases, only eight short of Lou Brock's NL record. Coleman's man-in-motion act obliterated Juan Samuel's 1984 rookie mark of 72 thefts. However, if not for the 1981 strike, Coleman's blistering performance might not have got him into the record books. In 1981, rookie Tim Raines stole 71 bases in just 88 games for the Expos. At that pace, Raines would have swiped 130 bases over a full season.

8.8 A. Juan Samuel of the Phillies

The 23-year-old second baseman displayed a dazzling blend of power and speed in his rookie season in 1985, amassing 36 doubles, 19 triples, 15 homers and 72 stolen bases. Samuel had three more solid years with the Phils before his production suddenly began to slip in 1988. Although he remained in the majors for another decade, Samuel did not develop into the force everyone thought he would.

8.9 C. Dwight Gooden

The Mets hurler was 20 when he copped the 1985 NL Cy Young, a scant 15 days younger than Fernando Valenzuela was when he took home the award in 1981. Gooden followed his mesmerizing rookie season with an even more stunning sophomore campaign, taking the pitcher's Triple Crown with a 24–4 record, 268 strikeouts and

THE STORMY YEARS

a 1.53 ERA. His ERA was the second-lowest since the deadball era, behind only Bob Gibson's microscopic 1.12 ERA in 1968. Gooden looked to be bound for the Hall of Fame, but drug problems derailed Doctor K's express train to Cooperstown.

LOWEST EARNED RUN AVERAGES (SINCE 1920)*

Player	Year	Team	IP	W	L	ERA
Bob Gibson	1968	Cardinals	304	22	9	1.12
Dwight Gooden	1985	Mets	276	24	4	1.53
Greg Maddux	1994	Braves	202	16	6	1.54
Luis Tiant	1968	Indians	258	21	9	1.60
Greg Maddux	1995	Braves	209	19	2	1.63
Spud Chandler	1943	Yankees	253	20	4	1.64
Dean Chance	1964	Angels	278	20	9	1.65
Carl Hubbell	1933	Giants	308	23	12	1.66

*CURRENT TO 1998

8.10 C. Fernando Valenzuela of the Dodgers

The one saving grace in the strike-marred 1981 season was the arrival of the charismatic Valenzuela. The rotund Mexican lefty won his first eight games as a starter in 1981, five of them by shutouts, and became a national sensation. Valenzuela opened the season with a 2–0 shutout against the Astros; in his second start against the Giants, he did not allow a run until there were two outs in the seventh inning. Combined with the 17⅔ shutout innings he racked up in relief late in 1980, Valenzuela pitched scoreless ball in his first 34⅓ innings in the majors, a big-league record. Although the Dodgers played only 110 games in 1981 because of the strike, Valenzuela twirled eight shutouts in 25 starts, the most goose eggs by a NL rookie in the 20th century.

8.11 C. Dave Winfield

A star pitcher and basketball player at the University of Minnesota, Winfield hit over .400, compiled a 13–1 won–lost record for the Golden Gophers and was voted MVP of the 1971 College World

Fernando Valenzuela: He had a dazzling rookie season in 1981.

Series. As well as being selected by the San Diego Padres in the fourth round of the 1973 baseball draft, he was also picked in the fifth round of the NBA draft by the Atlanta Hawks and in the sixth round of the ABA draft by the Utah Stars. Although Winfield did not play university football, the NFL's Minnesota Vikings thought enough of his athleticism to make him a seventh-round draft pick.

8.12 B. Mark Fidrych

With his long, curly, blond hair, his gangly frame and a habit of flapping his arms on the mound, Fidrych did bear a resemblance to the Sesame Street character "Big Bird." But the rookie's eccentric antics, such as talking to the ball, getting down on his hands and knees to landscape the pitching mound and jubilantly congratulating his infielders, would have had no impact if he hadn't been such an effective pitcher. Fidrych took the AL by storm in 1976, winning nine of his first ten decisions and becoming the first rookie since 1962 to be named the starting pitcher of an All-Star Game. He finished the season with a 19–9 record, 24 complete games and a 2.34 ERA. A financial godsend for Detroit, Fidrych drew 60 percent of the Tigers' total attendance in his starts and was personally responsible for more than a million dollars of the club's revenues. Tragically, he developed tendinitis in his pitching arm and won only ten more games before retiring in 1980.

8.13 A. Mike Schmidt

The career of baseball's greatest third baseman nearly didn't get off the ground. After two years in the minors, Schmidt was called up to the Phillies in 1973. He struggled badly, batting a meager .196, with 136 strikeouts in only 367 at-bats. He did, however, hit 18 homers, suggesting a potential for power. Schmidt realized he was swinging too hard and came to spring training the next year with a new attitude. Instead of trying to crush every pitch, he concentrated on picking good pitches to hit and swinging naturally. The strategy worked. He pounded 36 homers, drove in 116 runs and raised his average to .282. With his confidence restored, Schmidt never looked back, becoming the cornerstone around which the Phillies would build a championship-caliber team.

8.14 C. Wade Boggs

Many people unwisely dismissed Boggs's .349 average in 338 at-bats in 1982 as a fluke. He just didn't seem to have all the attributes needed to excel in the majors. He lacked power (five homers) and speed (one stolen base) and was a mediocre fielder. Boggs finished a distant third in the voting, behind winner Cal Ripken, and second-place finisher Kent Hrbek. But Boggs's rookie batting average was no mirage. He hit an AL-high .361 in 1983 and then won four more batting titles in the next five years. Even so, recognition was slow in coming. Boggs was not voted to the AL All-Star team until he had been in the league for four years.

8.15 A. Bob Horner

After being named 1978's College Player of the Year by *The Sporting News*, the Arizona State University star signed with the Atlanta Braves and debuted with the club in June of 1978. Even without any minor-league seasoning, Horner proved he was ready for the big time. The muscular third baseman belted a home run his third major-league at-bat and went on to swat 23 four-baggers and drive in 63 runs in only 323 at-bats, which was impressive enough for him to be voted NL Rookie of the Year.

8.16 D. Mark Eichorn of the Blue Jays

Eichorn's snaky, sidearm delivery baffled AL hitters in 1986 and helped him register 14 wins and ten saves in long relief for Toronto, along with a stellar 1.72 ERA. But just as baffling as the youngster's delivery was why Blue Jays manager Jimy Williams chose not to use Eichorn in the last couple of games of the season. He needed to pitch only five more innings to become the first reliever to win an AL ERA crown. Oddly, the lone reliever to win an NL ERA title—Hoyt Wilhelm of the 1952 New York Giants—was also a rookie. As it turned out, Roger Clemens led the AL in 1986 with a 2.48 ERA, and Eichorn soon faded into obscurity.

8.17 D. Todd Worrell of the Cardinals

A starting pitcher when he was drafted by St. Louis in the first round of the 1982 free-agent draft and for most of his minor-league career, Worrell made the switch to the bullpen in 1985. Called up by the pennant-winning Cardinals late in the year, he saved five games in 17 appearances and pitched effectively in the postseason. Installed as the Cardinals' closer in 1986, Worrell made 74 appearances and saved an NL-high 36 games, a record for rookies.

MOST SAVES BY ROOKIE RELIEVERS*

Pitcher	Year	Team	G	IP	W	L	ERA	SAV
Todd Worrell	1986	Cards	74	103	9	10	2.08	36
Rich Loiselle	1997	Pirates	72	72	1	5	3.10	29
Gregg Olson	1989	Orioles	64	85	5	2	1.69	27
Pete Ladd	1983	Brewers	44	49	3	4	2.55	25
Dick Radatz	1962	Red Sox	62	124	9	6	2.24	24
Doug Corbett	1980	Twins	73	136	8	6	1.98	23
Ken Tatum	1969	Angels	45	86	7	2	1.36	22
Rawley Eastwick	1975	Reds	58	90	5	3	2.60	22

*CURRENT TO 1998

8.18 **C. Lou Piniella**

Piniella was already a 26-year-old journeyman when he was voted Rookie of the Year with the Kansas City Royals in 1969. K.C. was the fifth club that had owned the rights to Piniella. He signed with the Cleveland Indians in 1962, was sent to the Washington Senators later that same year and then was traded to the Baltimore Orioles, for whom he played one game in 1964. Piniella was traded back to Cleveland in 1968, where he played six games and then was drafted by the Seattle Pilots in the 1968 expansion draft. The Pilots dealt him to the Royals in the spring of 1969.

LAST STOP ON THE LINE

All good things must come to an end, including the careers of baseball's most fabled performers. In some cases, the final whistle stop is a return to yesterday. Match the Hall of Famer with his last team.

(Answers are on page 139)

1. Willie Mays   _____   Cleveland Indians

2. Frank Robinson   _____   California Angels

3. Harmon Killebrew   _____   New York Mets

4. Tom Seaver   _____   Minnesota Twins

5. Joe Morgan   _____   New York Yankees

6. Rollie Fingers   _____   Milwaukee Brewers

7. Steve Carlton   _____   Kansas City Royals

8. Don Sutton   _____   Chicago Cubs

9. Catfish Hunter   _____   San Francisco Giants

10. Rod Carew   _____   Oakland Athletics

11. Willie McCovey   _____   Boston Red Sox

12. Ferguson Jenkins   _____   Los Angeles Dodgers

Carl Yastrzemski:
He led AL
outfielders in
assists a record
seven times.

Chapter Nine

OUT OF LEFT FIELD

The term "out of left field" is a popular metaphor for eccentric ideas and behavior. An intriguing explanation of how this phrase entered the lexicon is noted in the *Dickson Baseball Dictionary*. Evidently, the link between left field and oddness stems from the layout of Chicago's West Side Park, the original home of the Chicago Cubs. In the late 1800s, a mental hospital called the Neuropsychiatric Institute was located behind the park's left-field fence. Thus, in Chicago, when someone was described as being "out in left field," the implication was that they were behaving like the occupants of the institute, which was literally way out in left field.

In this chapter, we explore some of the era's zanier events and characters. *(Answers are on page 119)*

9.1 **Which pitcher admitted that he tossed a no-hitter while under the influence of LSD?**
A. Bill Stoneman of the Expos
B. Dock Ellis of the Pirates
C. Bill Lee of the Red Sox
D. LaMarr Hoyt of the White Sox

9.2 **A full-scale riot erupted when which team hosted a "Disco Demolition Night" during the 1979 season?**

A. The Chicago White Sox

B. The Cleveland Indians

C. The New York Mets

D. The Philadelphia Phillies

9.3 **Who was called a patriotic hero after he prevented two protesters from burning an American flag at Dodger Stadium in 1976?**

A. Rick Monday of the Cubs

B. Gary Matthews of the Giants

C. Richie Zisk of the Pirates

D. Dusty Baker of the Dodgers

9.4 **Who was Sidd Finch?**

A. The San Diego Chicken

B. Pete Rose's bookie

C. A fictional New York Mets pitcher

D. Charlie Finley's astrological consultant

9.5 **How did New York Yankees pitchers Fritz Peterson and Mike Kekich make headlines in 1973?**

A. They swapped wives

B. They sued George Steinbrenner

C. They were arrested for nude sunbathing

B. They ignited tear gas in the Yankee clubhouse

9.6 **Which owner seized a microphone at his team's home opener in 1974 and berated his club for its inept play?**

A. Ted Turner of the Braves

B. Ray Kroc of the Padres

C. Charlie Finley of the Athletics

D. George Steinbrenner of the Yankees

9.7 **Which Oakland A's player was offered a $2,000 bonus by owner Charlie Finley if he would agree to change his name?**

A. Sal Bando

B. Vida Blue

C. Mike Epstein

D. Mickey Klutts

9.8 **Why did Seattle Mariners manager Maury Wills receive a two-game suspension in 1981?**

A. He spit at an umpire

B. He used an illegal player

C. He ordered one of his pitchers to throw a bean ball

D. He secretly altered the size of the batter's box

9.9 **Which player was arrested for killing a seagull during a game at Toronto's Exhibition Stadium in 1983?**

A. Jim Rice of the Red Sox

B. Harold Baines of the White Sox

C. Dave Winfield of the Yankees

D. Rickey Henderson of the Athletics

9.10 **Which pitcher said, "If Nolan Ryan is the Ryan Express, I guess I'm the Marrakesh Express"?**

A. Steve Howe

B. Bill Lee

C. Tug McGraw

D. Don Stanhouse

9.11 **A busty blonde known as the "Kissing Bandit" attracted attention during the 1970s by running out on the field to kiss ballplayers. What was her name?**

A. Margo Adams

B. Della Delight

C. Morganna Roberts

D. Chesty Armstrong

9.12 Which team took the unusual step of naming its play-by-play broadcaster as its new manager in 1980?
A. The San Diego Padres
B. The Atlanta Braves
C. The Texas Rangers
D. The Boston Red Sox

9.13 Which owner attempted to end his team's losing streak by installing himself as manager?
A. Ted Turner of the Braves
B. Gene Autry of the Angels
C. Charlie Finley of the Athletics
D. George Steinbrenner of the Yankees

9.14 Which Rookie of the Year earned notoriety for such stunts as eating light bulbs and opening beer bottles with his eye socket?
A. John Montefusco of the Giants
B. Butch Metzger of the Padres
C. Ron Kittle of the White Sox
D. Joe Charboneau of the Indians

9.15 Which team's mascot was so unpopular that he retired because he feared being killed by hostile fans?
A. Pittsburgh's Parrot
B. Philadelphia's Fanatic
C. Atlanta's Chief Noc-a-homa
D. San Francisco's Crazy Crab

Answers

OUT OF LEFT FIELD

9.1 B. Dock Ellis of the Pirates

Ellis has only a hazy memory of tossing his lone no-hitter, a 2–0 victory over the San Diego Padres on June 12, 1970. "I can only remember bits and pieces of the game," he admitted in a 1984 interview. "I was psyched. I had a feeling of euphoria." No wonder. Ellis pitched the game under the influence of LSD, plus two other drugs—Dexamyl and Benzedrine—which he had taken to come down off the high. Ellis's performance, as no-hitters go, was sloppy—he walked eight Padres, hit one batter and allowed three stolen bases—but understandably so, because he believed the field was "melting around him." Pitching while in an altered state of consciousness was nothing new for Ellis, who confessed in his autobiography to using drugs, especially amphetamines and cocaine, during most of his 12-year career.

9.2 A. The Chicago White Sox

On July 12, 1979, White Sox owner Bill Veeck staged "Disco Demolition Night" at Comiskey Park. Between games of a double-header with the Detroit Tigers, Veeck planned to have disc jockey Steve Dahl blow up a dumpster filled with disco records as part of his national anti-disco crusade. Fans bringing disco albums for the demolition were admitted for 98 cents. Veeck anticipated a crowd of 35,000. Instead, 60,000 showed up. Things quickly got out of hand. By the midway point of the first game, Detroit's relief pitchers refused to warm up in the bullpen because of the volley of records and firecrackers cascading down from the upper deck. After the game, Dahl rode into center field in a military jeep, accompanied by a blonde "goddess of fire" called Lorelei, and set off the promised explosion. The crowd went berserk. Rowdies boogied onto the diamond, hijacked the batting cage, tore up hunks of sod, lit a bonfire in the outfield and partied for more than an hour, as the scoreboard futilely flashed the message, "Please return to your seats." When police finally quelled the riot, the umpires declared the field unplayable and forfeited the second game to Detroit. A shocked Veeck promised, "We'll make certain we don't try anything like this again."

9.3   A. Rick Monday of the Cubs

The most memorable catch of Monday's career occurred during the fourth inning of a game at Dodger Stadium on April 25, 1976, when the center fielder snatched an American flag away from two protesters just as they were about to set it afire. Monday delivered Old Glory safely to a security guard in the bullpen. The culprits, a man and his 11-year-old son, who were denouncing the treatment of Native Indians in the bicentennial year, were arrested and fined for trespassing. Monday was given a standing ovation by Dodger fans when he came to bat the next inning and was honored at a special day at Wrigley Field on May 4.

9.4   C. A fictional New York Mets pitcher

On April 1, 1985, *Sports Illustrated* published an article by George Plimpton, entitled "The Curious Case of Sidd Finch, Buddhist Pitcher." Finch was described as a Tibetan philosophy student who practised yoga, wore hiking boots on the mound and possessed a 160-mile-per-hour fastball. The article included photos of the young phenom secretly working out with the New York Mets, as well as quotes from Mets players. The story was an April Fool's prank, but some gullible readers were duped. *The St. Petersburg Times* even dispatched an investigative reporter to the Mets' training camp to write a follow-up piece.

9.5   A. They swapped wives

Not only did Yankee pitchers Mike Kekich and Fritz Peterson swap wives, they swapped lives: children, dogs, cars and homes. News of the bizarre lifestyle experiment became public during spring training in 1973 and resulted in a media circus. Yankees general manager Lee McPhail tried to make light of the situation, noting, "We may have to call off family day." Peterson and Kekich's careers went downhill in the wake of the distracting publicity, and both pitchers were soon traded. Fritz Peterson and Susan Kekich married; Mike Kekich and Marilyn Peterson's relationship did not survive.

9.6   B. Ray Kroc of the Padres

The Padres opened the 1974 season by losing their first three games to the Dodgers by lopsided 8–0, 8–0 and 9–2 scores. Those results didn't sit well with Kroc, who had just bought the team for $12 million. When the Padres displayed similar ineptitude in their home opener, falling behind 9–2 to the Houston Astros, the McDonald's hamburger tycoon blew his stack. Kroc seized the public-address microphone in the eighth inning and lambasted the team. "Ladies and gentlemen, I suffer with you," he told the stunned crowd. His outburst was interrupted by the sudden appearance of a naked fan racing across the field. "Get that streaker out of here," bellowed Kroc. "Throw him in jail!" Once the streaker had been removed, Kroc resumed his tirade, declaring, "I've never seen such stupid baseball playing in my life." Kroc would witness a lot more stupid play before 1974 was done. San Diego lost 102 games and finished last in the NL West for the sixth straight season.

9.7   B. Vida Blue

Charlie O. Finley tried to persuade Blue to change his name to True, believing it would add to the pitcher's box-office appeal. Blue refused, telling Finley, "I like my name the way it is. It's an unusual name as it is. And it was my father's name. It's Spanish, it means life." Finley persisted, offering him a $2,000 bonus to get it legally changed, but Blue held fast. A few days later, while warming up before a game, the young hurler was surprised to see himself listed as True Blue on the message board. He asked the A's publicity director to have it removed. Next, he discovered that the announcers had been told to refer to him as True Blue. Incensed with Finley's machinations, Blue told reporters, "If he thinks it's such a great idea why doesn't he change his name to True O'Finley?"

9.8 **D. He secretly altered the size of the batter's box**

Maury Wills was a terrific player but a terrible manager. As Bill James observed in *Sport* magazine: "Letting Maury Wills manage in the major leagues is like sending Bo Derek through cellblock A without a bodyguard." While piloting the Seattle Mariners in 1981, Wills was suspended for two games for "doctoring the batter's box." Umpires discovered that Wills had ordered his grounds-keeper to extend the batter's box an extra foot prior to a game against Oakland curveball pitcher Rick Langford. By the end of his 83-game stint as skipper, Wills's players were happy to lose, figuring it would speed up his departure.

9.9 **C. Dave Winfield of the Yankees**

On August 4, 1983, the Yankees found a new way to create controversy. In the middle of the fifth inning of a game with the Blue Jays at Toronto's Exhibition Stadium, Winfield short-hopped a sea gull with a warm-up throw, and the bird toppled over dead. Winfield removed his cap and held it over his heart as the ballboy ran onto the field with a white towel and carried the feathered corpse away. In response, the Toronto fans began to boo Winfield and pelt him with garbage. The heckling continued to the end of the game, which the Yankees won 3–1 on a Winfield homer. Afterward, police arrested the astonished Yankee on a charge of cruelty to animals, a offense that carried a maximum six-month jail sentence and a $500 fine. Winfield posted bail and left police headquarters to a barrage of photographers' flash bulbs. The charges were later dropped after Winfield convinced the crown attorney that the bird's death was an accident, but by then this fowl affair had taken on a life of its own. Winfield needed a police escort to get into the ballpark the next day, and when the Yankees moved on to Detroit, fans mockingly flapped their arms whenever he came to the plate. Manager Billy Martin offered the best line on the incident, noting, "That was the first time he hit the cutoff man all year."

9.10 **B. Bill Lee**

It's a baseball axiom that southpaw pitchers are flaky, but Lee's brand of weirdness appeared to spring from another dimension, which is why he was known as "the Spaceman." A free spirit who

Bill Lee: "The Ace from Outer Space."

read mystic philosophers like Gurdjieff and Ouspensky and who
described his mental state on the mound in Zen-like terms ("You
are the ball and the ball is you"), Lee was the first player to publicly
admit to using marijuana. He claimed he sprinkled it on his buck-
wheat pancakes each morning. At odds with the baseball establish-
ment on almost everything from artificial turf to designated hitters,
Lee disputed the notion that there was anything strange about
southpaws. "You have two hemispheres in your brain—a left side

123

and a right side. The left side controls the right side of your body, and the right controls the left half. Therefore, left-handers are the only people in their right minds."

9.11 C. Morganna Roberts

Roberts earned notoriety by jogging onto diamonds in the 1970s to plant big wet ones on ballplayers. She began her bussing career with Pete Rose in 1970 and went on to score with George Brett, Mike Schmidt, Nolan Ryan, Fred Lynn and others. Thanks to her awesome 60–24–39 statistics, Roberts created quite a stir, which helped her career as an exotic dancer. Arrested numerous times for trespassing, she introduced the gravity defense. "This woman, with a 112-pound body and a 15-pound chest, leaned over the rail to see a foul ball," explained her attorney. "Gravity took its toll, she fell out on the field, and the rest is history."

9.12 A. The San Diego Padres

In 1980, the Padres replaced skipper Roger Craig with team broadcaster Jerry Coleman, who was most famous for his mangled phrasemaking. Among his most memorable malaprops: "Rich Folkers is throwing up in the bullpen"; "McCovey swings and misses, and it's fouled back"; "George Hendrick simply lost that sun-blown pop up"; "Johnny Grubb slides into second with a stand-up double"; and "Ozzie Smith just made another play that I've never seen anyone else make before, and I've seen him make it more than anyone else ever has." Although Coleman played in the majors with the Yankees in the 1950s, he had no managerial experience. Whether it would have mattered is debatable, because the Padres had abysmal starting pitching. Reliever Rollie Fingers led the staff with 11 wins, as San Diego finished last in the NL West. By the year's end, Coleman couldn't wait to return to the broadcast booth, which he did after being fired.

9.13 A. Ted Turner of the Braves

On May 11, 1977, with the Braves in the throes of a 16-game losing streak, Ted Turner sent manager Dave Bristol on a scouting assignment and appointed himself interim manager. With Turner in uniform, the Braves made it 17 in a row, falling 2–1 to the Pirates. The next day, NL president Chub Feeney, citing a league rule that prohibits players and managers from owning stock in the team that employs them, ordered Turner out of the dugout. Coach Vern Benson assumed the controls and ended the losing streak, but the bleeding continued as the Braves dropped 101 games.

9.14 D. Joe Charboneau of the Indians

Dubbed "Super Joe" because of his assault on AL pitching in his rookie season in 1980—he hit .289 with 23 homers and 87 RBI—Charboneau became an overnight legend in Cleveland. Before the season was done, he would have a 500-member fan club and a song and a book written about him. Charboneau, who had earned money as a youth boxing bare-knuckled in boxcars—$20 for winning, $10 for losing—was renowned for his imperviousness to pain. He claimed to have fixed a broken nose with a vise grip, to have pulled out a rotten tooth with a pair of pliers and to have sliced a tattoo off his shoulder with a razor. During his rookie season, he entertained teammates by opening beer bottles with his eye socket. Whether Charboneau was merely eccentric is open to debate. His baseball talents mysteriously deserted him after 1980, and by 1982 he was back in the minors, never to return.

9.15 D. San Francisco's Crazy Crab

By the early 1980s, virtually every team in the majors had a mascot, except the San Francisco Giants. In 1984, Giants management jumped on the bandwagon by introducing the Crazy Crab. The ugly, orange-colored creature proved to be the most unpopular mascot in baseball history. At each game, when the Crab made its entrance, Giants fans would erupt in boos and hurl trash and beer. The grounds crew sprayed water hoses on the crustacean if it got too close to them. Before long, anti-Crab T-shirts began to appear. The mascot was eventually taken out of service because the man inside the costume feared for his safety.

T H E   R Y A N   R I D D L E

Nolan Ryan's career was puzzling in many respects. Despite being the greatest strikeout pitcher in baseball annals, he concluded his career with 324 wins and 292 losses, a winning percentage of .526. That's the worst of any 300-game winner. In fact, of the top 50 all-time winners, only two—Eppa Rixey and Jack Powell—have lower winning percentages than Ryan.

Of course, it's also true that Ryan pitched for a lot of mediocre teams. However, using a stat called Wins Above Team (WAT), it's possible to calculate how much Ryan's winning percentage was affected by the teams he played for. The stat, which is included in the book *Total Baseball*, indicates how many more games a particular pitcher won than an average pitcher would have won if both had pitched for the same team. Here's the formula:

$$\text{Pitcher's decisions} \times \frac{(\text{Pitcher's winning pct.} - \text{Team winning pct.})}{(2 - 2 \times \text{Team winning pct.})}$$

Ryan's career WAT is 11.3, which means that he won 11 more games than the average pitcher would have won. How does that compare with the lifetime marks of other pitchers? Not very well, as it turns out. Cy Young tops the chart at 99.7, followed by Walter Johnson (90.0), Grover Alexander (81.6), Christy Mathewson (64.9) and Lefty Grove (63.2). Ryan does not even make the top 100. If you limit the stat to include only post-1950 hurlers, Ryan is still far down the list. The following chart shows the top ten, not including still-active pitchers. Tom Seaver, who exceeded his team's winning percentage in 16 of his 20 seasons, is the runaway leader.

Pitcher	W	L	WAT
Tom Seaver	311	205	58.9
Whitey Ford	236	106	44.4
Juan Marichal	243	142	38.7
Phil Niekro	318	274	36.2
Steve Carlton	329	244	33.5
Bob Gibson	251	174	31.0
Sandy Koufax	165	87	30.6
Jim Palmer	268	152	30.2
Ferguson Jenkins	284	226	29.3
Ron Guidry	170	91	29.1

Ryan's low ranking would make more sense if his high strikeout rate was offset by allowing a lot of hits, but that's not the case — opposition batters hit an anemic .204 against Ryan, the lowest mark in history.

The one chink in Ryan's armor was his lack of control. He issued an average of 4.7 walks per nine innings. In fact, he led his league in walks a record eight times. If you add his free passes to the mix, you discover that his opponents' on-base percentage jumps to .310. In contrast, Sandy Koufax, another strikeout artist, had a career mark of .276.

If his control had been sharper, it's reasonable to assume that Ryan would have allowed fewer base runners and won more games. It's also possible that he would have pitched more complete games, because he would have been making fewer pitches, which might also have helped boost his win total. But this is all conjecture, and it doesn't entirely explain the discrepancy. Ryan remains an enigma, a great pitcher who fell short in a pitcher's central mission: winning games.

Reggie Jackson: His .755 World Series slugging average is the best of all time.

Chapter Ten

OCTOBER'S HEROES

Reggie Jackson once boasted, "The only reason I don't like playing in the World Series is I can't watch myself play." Jackson's arrogance often alienated people, but few players have delivered so consistently in big-game pressure. Between 1970 and 1983, no AL team *without* Jackson in the lineup won the World Series, while his teams—the A's, Yankees and Angels—won ten division crowns and five world titles. Jackson's most memorable postseason performance came in game six of the 1977 Series against the Dodgers, when he belted three homers on three straight swings off three different pitchers. Counting his clout in game five, the Yankee slugger hit four homers on four pitches and a record five in the Series. When the cheering was over, Jackson had acquired an indelible new nickname: "Mr. October." *(Answers are on page 133)*

10.1 Who was voted MVP of the 1969 series as the New York Mets upset the Baltimore Orioles?

A. Ron Swoboda

B. Tommy Agee

C. Tom Seaver

D. Donn Clendenon

10.2 Brooks Robinson's stellar defensive play helped Baltimore torpedo the Cincinnati Reds in the 1970 Series. Which Oriole led the offense, stroking nine hits, two homers and six RBI?

A. Boog Powell
B. Frank Robinson
C. Paul Blair
D. Brooks Robinson

10.3 What made game four of the 1971 Fall Classic between the Pirates and the Orioles a historic event?

A. It was the first World Series night game
B. Both managers were ejected for arguing calls
C. Roberto Clemente stroked a Series-record five hits
D. It featured the first grand-slam homer by a pitcher

10.4 Gene Tenace starred in Oakland's seven-game conquest of Cincinnati in 1972. How many of the A's 16 runs did Tenace either score or drive in?

A. Eight
B. Ten
C. 12
D. 14

10.5 Which Oakland player did A's owner Charlie Finley try to "fire" during the 1973 Series versus the Mets?

A. Dick Green
B. Mike Andrews
C. Ted Kubiak
D. Vic Davalillo

10.6 Which rookie Red Sox pitcher gave up the winning hit in the ninth inning of game seven of the 1975 Series with the Reds?

A. Roger Moret
B. Jim Burton
C. Dick Pole
D. Jim Willoughby

10.7 **Reggie Jackson's booming bat broke several World Series records in 1977, including most total bases. Which Yankee previously held the AL mark for most total bases in a Series?**
A. Babe Ruth
B. Lou Gehrig
C. Billy Martin
D. Mickey Mantle

10.8 **Which Kansas City Royals player did reliever Tug McGraw fan with the bases loaded in the ninth inning of game six, to nail down the 1980 Series for the Philadelphia Phillies?**
A. Amos Otis
B. George Brett
C. Darrell Porter
D. Willie Wilson

10.9 **How many Dodgers players shared the award for World Series MVP in 1981, as Los Angeles defeated the Yankees?**
A. None; a Yankee won the award
B. Two
C. Three
D. Four

10.10 **Which Cardinal won the MVP Award in the 1982 NLCS and the 1982 World Series, as St. Louis subdued the Braves and the Brewers?**
A. Willie McGee
B. Darrell Porter
C. Lonnie Smith
D. Keith Hernandez

10.11 **A contributing factor in the Cardinals' loss to the Royals in the 1985 Fall Classic was the absence of St. Louis leadoff hitter Vince Coleman. How had Coleman been injured?**
A. By getting hit by a foul ball
B. By punching a soap dispenser
C. By getting trampled by a runaway tarpaulin
D. By falling down the stairs while sleepwalking

10.12 In the tenth inning of game six of the 1986 Series, the Red Sox needed just one more out to clinch the Series. How many consecutive Mets batters did Boston fail to retire?

A. Two

B. Three

C. Four

D. Five

10.13 The Metrodome was supposed to provide the Minnesota Twins with a big home-field advantage in their 1987 tilt with the Cardinals. What was the Twins' final run count?

A. 33 at home, five on the road

B. 26 at home, 16 on the road

C. 19 at home, 19 on the road

D. 12 at home, 26 on the road

10.14 The turning point of the 1988 clash between the Dodgers and the A's was Kirk Gibson's clutch, ninth-inning, pinch-hit homer. In which game of the five-game Series did Gibson connect?

A. Game one

B. Game two

C. Game three

D. Game four

10.15 Which World Series record was set in game four of the 1989 Series between the A's and the Giants?

A. Most combined homers in one game

B. Most combined stolen bases in one game

C. Most combined runs in one game

D. Most combined strikeouts in one game

O C T O B E R ' S   H E R O E S

10.1 D. Donn Clendenon

In the year that a man first walked on the moon, the New York Mets won their first World Series. It is debatable which was the more miraculous event. Before 1969, the sad-sack Mets had never finished higher than second-last. But they won 100 games in 1969, overhauling the Chicago Cubs in September to secure the pennant. The Mets then deep-sixed the powerful Baltimore Orioles in five games to win the Series. Several Mets contributed to the upset, but the MVP Award went to Clendenon, one of the club's platoon players. The right-handed-hitting first baseman didn't see any action in the NLCS against the Braves, but he played in the Series because the Orioles kept starting left-handed pitchers. Clendenon responded by batting .357, with three homers and four RBI.

10.2 D. Brooks Robinson

Robinson's sizzling play at the hot corner gave the Reds' right-handed hitters nightmares in the 1970 Series, and evidently their manager, Sparky Anderson, shared their dreams. As Anderson told reporters during the Series, "I'm beginning to see Brooks in my sleep. If I dropped this paper plate, he'd pick it up on one hop and throw me out at first." Because of Robinson's defensive heroics, few recall that he was also the Birds' leading threat with the bat, hitting .429, and sparking several offensive salvos.

10.3 A. It was the first World Series night game

The lure of larger television revenues caused commissioner Bowie Kuhn to sanction the first World Series night game. Played at

133

Three Rivers Stadium on October 13, the contest drew a television audience of 50 million. The Orioles scored three runs in the first off jittery Pittsburgh starter Luke Walker, but rookie Bruce Kison came in to toss one-hit relief for six-and-a-third innings and the Pirates rallied to win 4–3, to knot the Series at two games each. Led by Roberto Clemente's hitting, the Corsairs would eventually triumph in seven games. Kuhn was so impressed with the results of his TV experiment that he announced that all weekday games of the 1972 Series would be played under the lights.

10.4 D. 14

Gene Tenace supplied almost all of Oakland's offense in the 1972 Series, batting .348, ripping four of the club's five homers and scoring five times and driving in nine runs. In all, he personally accounted for 14 of the team's 16 runs. No other A's player drove in more than one run. It was a startling display by Tenace, who had hit just five homers and batted .225 as the A's backup catcher during the regular season.

10.5 B. Mike Andrews

Sportswriter Jim Murray characterized Charlie Finley as "a self-made man who worships his creator." During the 1973 Series, it certainly appeared as if Finley was playing God. After A's second baseman Mike Andrews made two errors in the 12th inning of game two, opening the door to a four-run winning rally by the Mets, Finley tried to "fire" Andrews by putting him on the disabled list. To accomplish this he had the team physician compose a phony letter to commissioner Bowie Kuhn, stating that Andrews had a damaged shoulder. Finley coerced Andrews into going along with the fraud by threatening to have him blackballed from baseball. However, Kuhn refused to grant permission for the switch and Andrews stayed with the club. The A's players were infuriated by Finley's chicanery, but managed to ignore the distraction and took the Series in seven games.

10.6 B. Jim Burton

Many call the 1975 Boston–Cincinnati clash the greatest Series of all time, but it also featured some peculiar managerial decisions, none stranger than in game seven. Boston jumped out to a 3–0 lead in the deciding contest, but the Reds came back to tie it up on a two-run homer by Tony Perez in the sixth and an RBI single by Pete Rose in the seventh. After Red Sox skipper Darrell Johnson inexplicably lifted his top reliever, Jim Willoughby, for a pinch-hitter with two outs and no one on in the bottom of the eighth, he opted to send rookie reliever Jim Burton to the mound to face the mighty Reds in the ninth. Burton, who had only 53 innings of major-league experience, got two outs before allowing a Joe Morgan single that sent Kent Griffey racing home with the go-ahead run. Boston failed to score in the bottom of the ninth, and the Reds were world champions. For all intents and purposes, that marked the end of Burton's career (he pitched only two more innings), but Johnson lasted for another six seasons, never getting close to a ·World Series again.

10.7 **C. Billy Martin**
The Yankee manager had a front-row seat to watch Jackson light up Dodgers pitchers for 25 total bases on three singles, a double and five homers. Jackson's outburst broke the Series record of 24 shared by Duke Snider (1952) and Lou Brock (1968), and Martin's AL record of 23, set in the 1953 Fall Classic, when the second-sacker cracked seven singles, a double, two triples and two homers for the Yankees against the Brooklyn Dodgers.

MOST TOTAL BASES IN A WORLD SERIES*

Player	Year	Team	1B	2B	3B	HR	TB
Reggie Jackson	1977	Yankees	3	1	0	5	25
Willie Stargell	1979	Pirates	5	4	0	3	25
Duke Snider	1952	Dodgers	4	2	0	4	24
Lou Brock	1968	Cardinals	7	3	1	2	24
Paul Molitor	1993	Blue Jays	6	2	2	2	24
Billy Martin	1953	Yankees	7	1	2	2	23

*CURRENT TO 1998

10.8 D. Willie Wilson

Tug McGraw made four appearances in the 1980 Series, each one a cliffhanger. The Phillies closer preserved a one-run lead in the ninth inning of game one, lost game three in the tenth inning by giving up a two-out single, and then, in game five, with the Phils leading by one run, he loaded the bases in the ninth inning on three walks, before fanning Jose Cardenal for the final out. In game six, he relieved Steve Carlton in the eighth with Philadelphia up 4–0 and two men aboard. McGraw loaded the bases with a walk, then allowed one run to score on a sacrifice fly, before getting the third out. In the ninth, after getting one out, McGraw again loaded the sacks on a pair of singles and a walk to bring the potential winning run to the plate. He then retired Frank White on a pop fly and fanned Willie Wilson to end the Series. From the Phillies' standpoint, Wilson was the ideal man to have up in the situation. He hit a dismal .154 in the six-game affair, and his last strikeout was his 12th of the Series, a new record.

10.9 C. Three

In 1981, for the first time in history, there was a tie in the voting for Series MVP. Three Dodgers shared the award: Steve Garvey, Ron Cey and Pedro Guerrero. Garvey led L.A. with ten hits and a .417 average, Cey batted .350, with three homers and six RBI, while Guerrero chipped in with two dingers and seven RBI, five of them in the decisive sixth game as the Dodgers routed the Yankees 9–2.

10.10 B. Darrell Porter

The Missouri-born Porter was acquired by the Cardinals in 1981 to replace catcher Ted Simmons, who ironically had been traded to the Milwaukee Brewers. Porter struggled back in his home state and became a target of hecklers. But he redeemed himself in the 1982 postseason, hitting .556 in the Cards' sweep of the Atlanta Braves in the NLCS and contributing several key hits and defensive plays as the Redbirds beat the Brewers in the World Series.

10.11 C. By getting trampled by a runaway tarpaulin

Prior to the start of game four of the 1985 NLCS between the Cardinals and the Dodgers, rain began to fall in St. Louis. Outfielder

Vince Coleman was walking off the field after doing some exercises, when a member of the grounds crew activated the automatic tarpaulin machine. The 150-foot-long cylinder began rolling across the field and slammed into Coleman, knocking him to the ground. The St. Louis speedster suffered a chipped bone in his left knee that sidelined him for the rest of the postseason. Without Coleman, who had stolen 110 bases during the season, the Cardinals' running game was severely hampered. They swiped only two bases, compared with six by the Royals in their seven-game defeat.

10.12 C. Four

Boston was leading the Mets 5–3 with two outs and no one on base in the bottom of the tenth inning of game six, when it all suddenly slipped away. Gary Carter nicked pitcher Calvin Schiraldi for a single to left. Kevin Mitchell rapped a pinch single up the middle. Ray Knight blooped a hit to center, scoring Carter and moving Mitchell to third. Schiraldi was replaced by Bob Stanley, who came in to pitch to Mookie Wilson. With the count 2–2, Stanley uncorked a wild pitch that allowed Mitchell to score to tie the game and enabled Knight to advance to second. Wilson then hit a routine grounder to Bill Buckner at first. Buckner let the ball roll under his glove, and Knight scampered home with the winning run. The Mets had sent four batters to the plate and scored three runs on three singles, a wild pitch and an error. Two days later, New York completed its astounding comeback, beating the BoSox 8–5 to take the Series.

10.13 A. 33 at home, five on the road

When the Minnesota Twins beat the St. Louis Cardinals in the 1987 World Series, many noted how much better the Twins performed at the Metrodome. Cardinals shortstop Ozzie Smith suspected that the Twins benefited from something more than simply the raucous home crowd. According to Smith, Cardinals fly balls suddenly died when they reached a certain point in the outfield. Yet the balls the Twins hit would reach the same point and continue to carry. Smith was convinced that the indoor stadium's air blowers were secretly being turned on when the Twins were at bat and turned off when the Cardinals were at the plate. Lest we dismiss Smith's theory as simply hot air, it's worth noting that Minnesota hit six homers and scored 33 runs in the four games at the Metrodome, in contrast to only one homer and five runs in the three games at St. Louis' Busch Stadium.

10.14 A. Game one

The first sign that the 1988 Series would feature some unusual events came in the first inning of game one, when the Dodgers' Mickey Hatcher hit a home run, matching his entire total for the season. The next surprise came with Oakland leading 4–3 in the ninth, with two outs and nobody on base, when A's closer Dennis Eckersley walked light-hitting Dodgers' DH Mike Davis. Eckersley had walked just 11 batters in 72 ⅔ innings during the season, and Davis had hit only .196 during the year. With pitcher Alejandro Pena due to bat, Dodgers manager Tommy Lasorda summoned Kirk Gibson to pinch hit. Gibson, who was hobbled by a pulled hamstring, wasn't even supposed to play. Wincing with every swing, Gibson doggedly worked the count to 3–2. On the next pitch, he connected with an Eckersley slider, sending the ball into the right-field bleachers and turning Dodger Stadium into a madhouse. As Gibson limped around the bases to be mobbed at home plate, TV announcer Vin Scully said: "In a year that has been so improbable, the impossible has happened." Gibson would not have another at-bat in the Series, but the gritty Dodgers went on to down the powerhouse A's in five games.

10.15 A. Most combined homers in one game

On October 27, 1989, after a ten-day delay caused by an earthquake that registered 7.1 on the Richter scale, the Bay City series between Oakland and San Francisco reconvened at Candlestick Park, where fans witnessed another series of big jolts. This time it was the bats of the A's and Giants that supplied the reverberations. The A's belted five homers, and the Giants added two as Oakland pounded out a 13–7 win to take a 3–0 lead in the Series. The seven homers set a new Series record for most round-trippers in one game.

Game Answers

Game 1:
Baseball Titles
1.	H	7.	C
2.	G	8.	J
3.	E	9.	D
4.	I	10.	A
5.	F	11.	L
6.	B	12.	K

Game 2:
You Can Quote Me
1. Pete Rose
2. Graig Nettles
3. Gaylord Perry
4. Dick Allen
5. Bobby Bonds
6. Mickey Lolich
7. Billy Martin
8. Yogi Berra
9. Earl Weaver
10. Dan Quisenberry
11. George Brett
12. Bob Uecker
13. Rickey Henderson
14. Harmon Killebrew
15. Bill Lee
16. Reggie Jackson

Game 3:
Mound Magicians
1. Nolan Ryan
2. Phil Niekro
3. Jim Kaat
4. Tom Browning
5. Jim Palmer
6. Steve Carlton
7. Ferguson Jenkins
8. Don Sutton
9. Tom Seaver
10. Bill Gullickson
11. Randy Jones
12. Gaylord Perry

Game 4:
Higher or Lower?
1. A. 23 (5)
   B. 21
2. A. 1,730 (5)
   B. 1,383
3. A. 145 (5)
   B. 121
4. A. 385
   B. 414 (10)
5. A. 10 (5)
   B. 8
6. A. .267
   B. .292 (10)
7. A. 0
   B. 4 (10)
8. A. 3
   B. 4 (10)
9. A. 18
   B. 21 (10)
10. A. 242 (5)
    B. 222
Mystery number = 75

Game 5:
Trading Places
1. Dave May
2. Charlie Williams
3. Ken Landreaux
4. Tom Lawless
5. Jim Fregosi
6. Rick Wise
7. Mike Caldwell
8. Neil Allen
9. Dave Tomlin
10. Ivan Dejesus

Game 6: Counterfeit Credentials
1. Don Baylor
2. Tom Seaver
3. Tony Perez
4. Alan Trammell
5. Eddie Murray
6. Frank Robinson
7. Mickey Lolich
8. Jose Cruz
9. Nolan Ryan
10. Juan Marichal

Game 7:
Closing the Deal
1. Dave Righetti
   (1986 Yankees)
2. Dan Quisenberry
   (1983 Royals)
3. Bruce Sutter
   (1984 Cardinals)
4. Jeff Reardon
   (1988 Twins)
5. John Hiller
   (1973 Tigers)
6. Rollie Fingers
   (1978 Padres)
7. Sparky Lyle
   (1972 Yankees)
8. Goose Gossage
   (1980 Yankees)
9. Kent Tekulve
   (1978 Pirates)

Game 8:
Last Stop on the Line
1. New York Mets
2. Cleveland Indians
3. Kansas City Royals
4. Boston Red Sox
5. Oakland Athletics
6. Milwaukee Brewers
7. Minnesota Twins
8. Los Angeles Dodgers
9. New York Yankees
10. California Angels
11. San Francisco Giants
12. Chicago Cubs

ACKNOWLEDGEMENTS

The author gratefully acknowledges the help of photo researchers W.C. Burdick of the National Baseball Hall of Fame and Steve Gietschier of *The Sporting News,* editor John Eerkes, designer Peter Cocking, Rob Sanders and Terri Wershler of Greystone Books, Candice Lee, Brian Banks, and the many baseball writers whose brilliant prose has helped to illuminate the game.

PHOTO CREDITS

ABOUT THE AUTHOR

Kerry Banks is an award-winning journalist and sports columnist. He is also the author of *The Glory Years: Old-Time Baseball Trivia* and *The Babe Ruth Era: Old-Time Baseball Trivia,* and the co-author of *Classic Hockey Trivia* and *Ultimate Hockey Trivia.*